# TAKING CARE OF WHAT WE HAVE

## PARTICIPATORY NATURAL RESOURCE MANAGEMENT ON THE CARIBBEAN COAST OF NICARAGUA

Patrick Christie, David Bradford, Ray Garth, Bonifacio González, Mark Hostetler ,
Oswaldo Morales, Roberto Rigby, Bertha Simmons, Eduardo Tinkam, Gabriel Vega,
Ronnie Vernooy, Noreen White

CENTRO DE INVESTIGACIONES Y DOCUMENTACION DE LA COSTA ATLANTICA
Bilwi-Bluefields-Managua, Nicaragua

INTERNATIONAL DEVELOPMENT RESEARCH CENTRE
Ottawa-Cairo-Dakar-Johannesburg-Montevideo-Nairobi-New Delhi-Singapore

**Published jointly by the**

Centre for Research and Documentation of the Atlantic Coast
AP A-189, Managua, Nicaragua (http://apc.nicarao.org.ni/cidca)

**and the**

International Development Research Centre
PO Box 8500, Ottawa, ON, Canada K1G 3H9 (http://www.idrc.ca)

© Centro de Investigación y Documentación de la Costa Atlántica (CIDCA) 2000


**Canadian Cataloguing in Publication Data**

Main entry under title :

Taking care of what we have : participatory natural resource management on the Caribbean
Coast of Nicaragua

Co-published by the Centre for Research and Documentation of the Atlantic Coast
(CIDCA).
ISBN 0-88936-925-9

1. Conservation of natural resources — Nicaragua — Atlantic Coast.
2. Coastal ecology — Nicaragua — Atlantic Coast.
3. Atlantic Coast (Nicaragua) — Environmental aspects.
I. Christie, Patrick.
II. Centro de Investigaciones y Documentación de la Costa Atlántica (Nicaragua).
III. International Development Research Centre (Canada)

QH541.5C65T34 2000          577'.51'0972853          C00-980145-6

Front cover photos by Patrick Christie and Stanley Honda

# CONTENTS

# FOREWORD

The International Development Research Centre (IDRC) is very happy to be a partner with the Centre for Research and Documentation of the Atlantic Coast/ Central American University (CIDCA/UCA) in the Coastal Area Monitoring Project and Laboratory (CAMPlab) and in the publication of this book. This book is one output of an ongoing project that started in 1993.

What is in a title? To my mind this title is particularly appropriate as it clearly embodies the long term objectives of this project: taking care of what we have, or, in a more formal sense, beginning the process of managing one's resources. This is (and will continue to be) one of the most vexing challenges facing those of us concerned about sustainable development of natural resources. Development workers, resource managers, researchers, funding agency staff, and hopefully some community leaders will all find this material illustrative in terms of principles as well as practical experiences on the ground; and as an example of making sustainable development work under a demanding set of conditions.

This book provides a very interesting case study of the management of coastal resources, both terrestrial and aquatic, in and around the Pearl Lagoon on the Caribbean coast of Nicaragua. It is useful to be reminded that coastal zones are areas of transition where oceans meet land, where salt water meets fresh water and where the natural resource base is both productive and diverse. As the reader will see, the inhabitants of this coastal ecosystem have adopted a variety of strategies in terms of use of these resources. Research results to date document a move from a major historical focus on land-based, mainly farming activities to more recent increased harvesting of the abundant aquatic resources such as shrimp, lobster, and fin fish in this unique lagoon system. Increasingly, driven by the globalization agenda, these aquatic products are being marketed at the regional and international levels.

Signs of resource system stress are now beginning to show up — expressed both by traditional knowledge indicators as well as more formal science-based results. Studies leading to management, at least in any more formal sense, are only recently being undertaken, in part through the CAMPlab project. This book represents a new approach to the study and future management of this complex of resource systems that to date have been relatively unknown particularly in the Caribbean region. Questions related to "who" and "when" (supplemented with the how, what, and where) are examined under a participatory action research program.

There are a variety of broader issues that are important to highlight. As I mentioned, the authors argue forcibly for the need to involve *from the outset* the groups, who most actively use and depend on these resources. This involvement should be both in the setting of the research-for-development agenda as well as the actions that follow in terms of improved management programs. Although seemingly self-evident, this type of early involvement, or involvement at all, has not been the norm in many such past activities.

***The need for persistence:*** We need to be reminded periodically that development is a long-term process. This project started small and has grown over the last 7 years, but it is recognized that there is still a considerable distance to go to reach the objectives of improved management of the Pearl Lagoon coastal ecosystems.

We also need to recognize that a variety of levels impinge on the development process. In most coastal resource management plans, adequate emphasis has not been placed on the local level. The authors argue for a greater ***emphasis on the local community level*** — involving the users (indigenous, ethnic, migrant, etc.) from the start of the process, through the use of participatory action research. There now exists in the communities around the Pearl Lagoon both an awareness of the value of community involvement and a core of trained community members who are skilled in its use. This group, under the umbrella of the evolving system of regional autonomy in Nicaragua, is increasingly arguing for a more equitable system for management.

The CAMPlab project has led to the development of new ***interdisciplinary research approaches*** with a special emphasis on research that links the natural and social science paradigms by examining both the people and the natural resources as part of one system. The subsequent chapters provide operational experiences and methods on how to better understand the use of coastal resources as seen by the main users. For instance, the research team has developed a monitoring program and database on the people and their uses of land and water resources including how these are changing over time. The latter issue is particularly important as mechanisms to monitor these temporal changes must incorporate an ecosystem view in which upstream to downstream impacts are critical.

For the future, as this work moves into a broader development phase, new challenges are already suggested in terms of corresponding institutional and organizational changes. The need for increased emphasis on the local level involves clear trade-offs in this work, particularly the high transaction costs required to ensure adequate representation. More experience in Pearl Lagoon and from other case studies over a longer time period will be important in providing insights into how to balance these trade-offs.

*F. Brian Davy*
*Research Manager*
*International Development Research Centre*
*Ottawa, Canada*

# ACKNOWLEDGEMENTS

This has been a long and interesting road. As Paulo Freire and Myles Horton have remarked, "We make the road by walking." We take this to mean that what makes participatory action research challenging, and so effective, is that it is not a predetermined road. Rather, it is a creative endeavour. It depends on the commitment of people to a process they believe in and is shaped by external conditions that resist and support it. The CAMPlab project and this book, in particular, are the products of the efforts of many committed people who bring an exciting diversity of skills and experiences to bear on the problems of resource management in Pearl Lagoon, Nicaragua.

We acknowledge the technical support generously provided by Ken MacKay and Brian Davy on behalf of the International Development Research Centre and by Nestor Nepal on behalf of Norwegian Popular Aid. We also acknowledge Professor Hugo Sujo and the late Karen Levy of the Center for Research and Documentation of the Atlantic Coast, who tirelessly supported this project through very challenging times.

CAMPlab has enjoyed considerable support from technical advisors and people interested in community-based resource management and participatory action research. In particular, Joe Ryan and Edmundo Gordon demonstrated a deep commitment to Nicaragua and CAMPlab in various ways. We thank Gary Newkirk, Veronika Brzeski, and Becky Field at Dalhousie University in Canada for exposing CAMPlab staff to new perspectives. John Vandermeer and Ivette Perfecto of the University of Michigan in the United States generously invited CAMPlab staff to participate in forest ecology field courses. Davyd Greenwood and Orlando Fals Borda provided timely and sage advice along the way concerning the ins and outs of participatory action research.

Locally, CAMPlab has benefited from strong and necessary support from important coastal leaders. In particular, we would like to acknowledge Carl "Fritz" Tinkam, Miguel González, and Faran Dometz for their commitment to a process that they believe will benefit coastal communities.

The book links together the writing contributions of different members of the CAMPlab research team and two associated researchers from the USA and Canada, under the editorial direction of Ronnie Vernooy, the program officer responisble for the project at the International Development Research Centre, Canada.

Sandra Garland, Alvaro Rivas, Bernard Hoareau, and Bill Carman deserve special acknowledgement for the preparation of this book.

Finally, and most important, we acknowledge the people of Pearl Lagoon who worked selflessly to improve their communities and their environment. The voluntary participants in CAMPlab represent the greatest inspiration of all. Salomon Archibold, Winston Brown, Chris DeSouza, Armando Douglas, Granville Garth, Samuel Hodgson, Junita Howard, Guillermo Ingram, Silvia López, Luis Montalban, Manuela Morales, and Marnie Tinkam are examples of the committed participants who have given generously of themselves for the sake of their communities. You are an inspiration that reminds us of the capacity of human generosity.

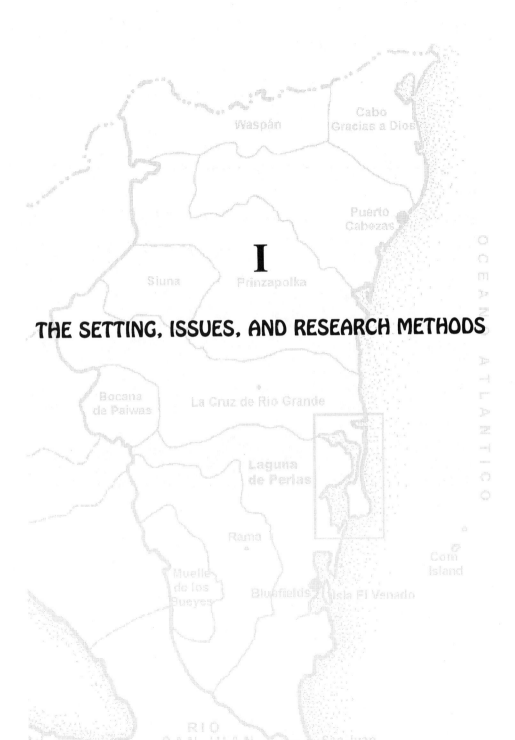

# I

# THE SETTING, ISSUES, AND RESEARCH METHODS

Photo: CIDCA

# 1.    THE SETTING, ISSUES, AND RESEARCH METHODS

*Ronnie Vernooy, Patrick Christie, David Bradford,
Ray Garth, Bonifacio González, Mark Hostetler,
Oswaldo Morales, Roberto Rigby, Bertha Simmons,
Eduardo Tinkam, Gabriel Vega, Noreen White*

Coastal regions around the world are under enormous pressure resulting from rapid population expansion, increased commercialization and overexploitation of aquatic resources, downstream effects of deforestation and pollution, and private-interests' encroachment on communally owned resources. In this book, we offer detailed insights into the problems surrounding natural resource management and possible alternatives in a specific coastal region — Pearl Lagoon on the Caribbean coast of Nicaragua.

## Focusing on the Caribbean coast

The Caribbean or Atlantic (east) coast of Nicaragua is a complex mosaic of interrelated coastal and terrestrial ecosystems and multi-ethnic communities that extends approximately 500 km from Honduras to Costa Rica. It contains one of the largest remaining areas of tropical lowland rainforest in Central America and one of the most pristine fisheries of the Caribbean basin. Together these systems make this an area of impressive biodiversity. The coast's labyrinth of lagoons and rivers provide an important habitat for fish and shrimp. Offshore, a wide continental shelf contains beds of sea grasses and coral reefs that harbour sea turtles, shrimp, lobster, and fish.

The Pacific and Caribbean coasts of Nicaragua are ecological and culturally different. The vast majority of the people on the Pacific coast are Spanish-speaking Mestizos, descendants of Spanish and indigenous peoples. The lowlands of the Pacific were covered primarily by dry, deciduous forests that were converted to agricultural land, first by indigenous populations, then more completely by European settlers.

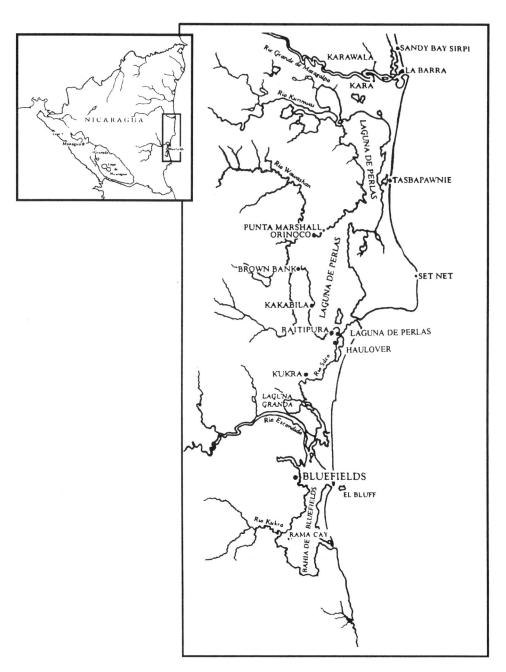

***Figure 1. Map of Nicaragua, showing the Caribbean coast.***

A north-south ridge of mountains divides the Pacific lowlands from the Caribbean lowlands. The Caribbean coast region ("the coast") comprises all the land east of the central mountain ridge (see Fig. 1). Its population density is lower than that of the rest of Nicaragua, with almost 0.4 million people in an area that covers about 56% the country (INEC 1996). The region is divided by the Río Grande de Matagalpa into two politically autonomous regions: the Región Autónoma Atlántico Sur (Southern Autonomous Atlantic Region) or RAAS in the south and the Región Autónoma Atlántico Norte (Northern Autonomous Atlantic Region) or RAAN in the north.

After years of discussion and negotiation with numerous communities along the coast, in 1987, the National Assembly of Nicaragua passed the Autonomy Statute for the Regions of the Atlantic coast of Nicaragua (Law No. 28). This landmark piece of legislation recognized Nicaragua as a multi-ethnic society and acknowledged the need for drastic change to improve living conditions of those oppressed due to their ethnicity. The statute reaffirmed that the coast is an integral part of Nicaragua, and the RAAN and RAAS were granted the following special rights: cross-cultural and bilingual education, communal lands, the defense of cultural heritage and traditional forms of organization, direct benefits from the area's natural resources within national development plans, and locally-elected regional councils that will represent the coast in the national government and participate, with national agencies, in planning the use of the area's natural resources.

The revised National Constitution of 1995 also recognized the multi-ethnicity of Nicaragua (Article 8), the official use of languages other than Spanish on the coast (Article 11), the need for cross-cultural education (Article 121), and the right of indigenous people (Costeños) to preserve their culture and benefit from their natural resources (Article 180).

## The study area

Pearl Lagoon (or Laguna de Perlas) is about halfway along the coast between Honduras and Costa Rica (Fig. 2), about 55 km (or 1.5 h by motorboat) north of Bluefields, the capital of the RAAS and the major city on the coast. The basin surrounding the lagoon covers about 5200 km$^2$ and represents a microcosm of the coast, with its ethnic and religious diversity, rich endowment of natural resources, and demographics.

Twelve communities are situated around the basin. The populations of the town of Pearl Lagoon, Haulover, Brown Bank, La Fe, San Vicente (also known as Square Point), Marshall Point, and Orinoco are mainly English-speaking; residents of Kakabila, Raitipura, Awas, Tasbapauni, and Set Net Point are either bilingual English–Miskitu or speak English only (Jamieson 1999, p. 22). Pueblo Nuevo, located

**5**

upstream on the Wawashang River, is Spanish speaking. Many people in the lagoon area may also speak Spanish, but not usually in everyday conversation.

Most of these small coastal communities have less than 500 inhabitants; their total population is about 6500. They differ depending on the occupation (a mix of fisheries, agriculture, forestry, and trade) and ethnicity of their inhabitants, but they share an impression of remote tranquility. In general, small homes are clustered out along the shore of the lagoon. Large fruit trees are scattered in open, grassy yards that are occupied by roaming cattle. All the communities have wharves, but the majority of the small boats are moored along the shore. Transportation among the settlements and between them and the outside world is necessarily by boat: there are no roads.

## Pressure on people and resources

The coast is still rich in natural resources, although the sociopolitical situation significantly limits the potential for their sustainable management (Walker 1997). Currently, many factors are affecting patterns of natural resource use.

The armed conflict that took place in the country during the 1980s and into the early 1990s is still affecting the infrastructure and social fabric of coastal communities. Reconstruction has been slow. Many coastal residents, young men in particular, have left the area, many never to return.

In 1988, Hurricane Joan changed the landscape dramatically, destroying parcels of forest, eroding coasts, causing the death and dispersal of fauna, and resulting in huge forest fires during the 1989 dry season that followed. Although the impact of the hurricane is difficult to isolate, alterations to the forests, agricultural lands, and waterways have been documented (Vandermeer and Perfecto 1991; Vandermeer 1992; Vernooy 1992).

The agricultural frontier, which is advancing from the west, has reached the headwaters of the rivers that feed the Pearl Lagoon basin. This is creating tension between the mainly Mestizo farmers and the non-Mestizo, basin residents. Displaced landless peasants from the interior are deforesting extensive communal lands that cover a range of ecosystems — lowland rainforest, swamp forest, pine savanna, and mangrove forests — not only creating conflict, but also increasing sedimentation rates in rivers.

The rapid influx of transnational corporations moving into the area to exploit forest and fisheries resources is having a direct impact on the approximately 1600 people engaging in fishing and shrimp trapping (Van der Hoeven et al. 1996). Fish export companies, some with the direct assistance or other benefits offered by "development" projects, are encouraging rapid increases in fish extraction.

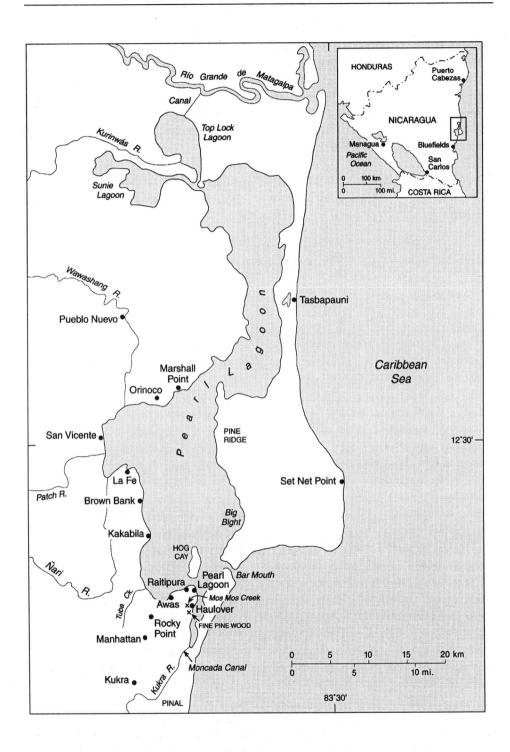

*Figure 2: Location of Pearl Lagoon, showing the towns and rivers in the study area.*

On the political scene, power struggles between opposing parties, as well as battles between coastal groups and the national government based in Managua — mainly arising from the latter's lack of political will — have made implementation of the autonomy law very difficult. In addition, the decision-making processes defined in the autonomy law are under heavy pressure due to centralized policymaking rules and regulations pushed through by Nicaragua's current neoliberal government.

Finally, the drug trade is having a significant impact on the region, as the coast is increasingly being used as a route to the United States by Colombian drug dealers.

## A project is born

In 1993, these pressures and a desire to address their underlying causes gave rise to an initiative to focus on issues surrounding the use of natural resources in the Pearl Lagoon basin. Under the leadership of Patrick Christie, then a master's student at the University of Michigan, and Roberto Rigby, a Nicaraguan marine biologist with the Centro de Investigaciones y Documentación de la Costa Atlántica (CIDCA), a 6-month period of exploratory research resulted in the identification by local people of the need for a management plan for the basin's natural resources. The breakdown of traditional mechanisms of resource management, caused by the war and the rapid transformation of the subsistence economy into an increasingly commercial and market-driven one, had led to a situation in which resources were depleted on a scale and in a rhythm that was causing major concerns.

In 1994, the project entered a formal research phase, with emphasis on the most important aspects of the coastal environment that were identified by the habitants: the lagoon fisheries, the pine forest, and the freshwater rivers. The project also expanded geographically; in addition to the town of Pearl Lagoon, three other communities became directly involved — Kakabila, Orinoco, and Marshall Point. An interdisciplinary research team, formed under the leadership of CIDCA, included "communal" investigators, i.e., women and men from the local communities with an interest in studying the issues related to management of the natural resource base. Roberto Rigby and Patrick Christie continued to be involved in a leadership role, although management tasks were increasingly taken over by other team members. In 1998, when Roberto Rigby left to study abroad, Bertha Simmons became the new project leader.

Other researchers, including Mark Hostetler, who is currently pursuing a PhD degree at York University in Toronto, Canada, joined the project in 1997, carrying out fieldwork on specific issues relevant to the management of the natural resources.

Thus, over the course of 6 years, this initiative, originally named the Coastal Area Monitoring Project (CAMP; later called CAMPlab when a laboratory unit was added [see Roustan and Robinson 1997, pp. 2–6; Christie 1999, pp. 271–281]) has grown to include dozens of individuals from the 12 lagoon communities and seven full-time staff. Local people are involved in monitoring pine savannas, fish populations, and water quality using qualitative and quantitative methods. They are also developing stronger community-level institutions. The goal has been to develop a knowledge base to inform a formal management regime for the area's coastal resources. Eventually local residents, through CAMPlab, became involved in the development of a fisheries management plan and a pine savanna management plan. They also initiated reforestation of denuded pine savanna.

## Participatory action research

From the start, CAMP/CAMPlab adopted a participatory action research (PAR) approach that is described and assessed in this book. PAR is based on four key features (Christie 1999):

1. The traditional, positivist scientific manner of generating knowledge, while valid for certain objectives and undoubtedly powerful, is considered to be only one of a variety of acceptable mechanisms for generating knowledge. Participatory action researchers argue against conducting only so called "valid, objective," reductionistic (social) science. What they argue for is the need to produce results that contribute to the reduction of oppression and social problems. In their view, the traditional scientific method is not the best means for generating accurate information in oppressive circumstances.

2. Such an approach requires the transformation of the traditional subject–object relationship into a subject–subject one. This insight is perhaps the core of Paulo Freire's (1992, 1993) method for understanding and addressing oppression: people are no longer merely the *objects* of the knowledge creation process, rather they act as *subjects* creating their own useful knowledge. As creators of knowledge, they begin creating an improved social reality by addressing oppressive relationships.

   In practice, this implies a completely different relationship between the professional researcher and "the researched" than that of traditional scientific research. Research becomes a co-learning process in problem identification, data collection, analysis, and action. Ideally, each player or stakeholder in the research process brings his or her special skills and knowledge to bear on the problem as a way of increasing the level of understanding by looking at it from different perspectives.

3.    From these characteristics of PAR follows the importance placed on process as well as outcomes (for an insightful discussion of the concept of participation as both means and end in itself, see McAllister 1999). Some practitioners call for the development of a sociopolitical process with which the oppressed can identify (Fals-Borda and Rahman 1991). Others describe the process as one of dis-indoctrination and detachment from the myths of society that maintain oppression (Vio Grossi 1981). Freire (1993) aptly describes these myths as veils hanging before the eyes of the oppressed.

4.    The link between reflection or analysis and action is better known as the concept of praxis. Freire (1993) explains that praxis implies no dichotomy by which reflection and action are defined into separate stages; rather they should occur simultaneously. The practical importance of praxis is that it suggests that one should move between reflection and action as a means of increasing critical consciousness in an iterative way. As participants in the process pass through cycles of "problematization" to action, increased critical consciousness is gained. However, this is a slow and not necessarily linear process that must be nurtured. It also depends on constancy and creativity in the face of inevitable adversity.

## Objectives of participatory action research

These four cornerstones of PAR support its two major objectives: empowerment and social change. Action research practitioners work with marginalized people to jointly assess oppressive social relationships and to generate information that can be used to develop solutions to practical problems. In the face of adversity, the action of gathering knowledge is viewed as an empowering first step. It is also democratizing in the sense that it demonstrates that all people can take part in research as true stakeholders.

Empowerment also implies articulation between bodies of knowledge. In a world transformed by science and technology, the knowledge of the oppressed has been widely designated by elites as inferior and excluded from what they consider the realm of legitimate, verifiable knowledge.

Although the link between research and action is generally acknowledged by practitioners in the abstract sense, there is no agreement on the form that this action takes. Some argue that political action is a logical outcome to challenge the existing power structure that perpetuates oppression. Others are willing to work within the existing power structure to reach more pragmatic goals.

From 1993, CAMP was funded and supported by Canada's International Development Research Centre (IDRC). The project follows a trajectory of support to PAR, as one approach to realize IDRC's mission, which is captured in the phrase "empowerment through knowledge." Through financial and technical support to applied, development-oriented research projects, IDRC aims to provide the means for people to

❖     study their own situation, problems, constraints, and potential;

❖     gather and analyze relevant data concerning this situation;

❖     propose action and execute plans and projects that will solve identified problems and improve the livelihoods of the people, efficiently and effectively;

❖     assess the outcomes of the research and intervention process and learn from these outcomes for the benefit of future projects and programs.

These objectives are very much in line with the general goals of PAR, which, as outlined above, emerged to make science respond more directly to the ideas and needs of the people most affected by poverty, oppression, and resource degradation. However, this does not mean only the development of improved technologies. Apart from new and improved technologies and increased capacity to do research, more functional forms of organizations and better policies are also seen as responses to the problems of marginalization. In other words, PAR is seen as both a process to improve understanding of the complexities of social life and as a means to provide a more sound base for action.

As the project described in this book illustrates, at the heart of this approach is a collective effort by professional researchers and nonprofessional researchers to

❖     set research priorities and identify key problems and issues;

❖     analyse the causes that underlie these problems and issues and

❖     take action to find both short-term and long-term solutions to the identified problems.

Such an approach is expected to have a positive impact on effectiveness, in terms of increased use and acceptability of research results; efficiency (making better use of resources, lower costs of project execution and delivery of results); and capacity (the ability to do research through increased conceptual and methodological expertise).

PAR for sustainable natural resource management is very much about the building and strengthening of local organizations. Through these organizations, local people become empowered and empower themselves to have a greater say in decision-making about the use and long-term management of soil, trees, water, and animals. People perceive this clearly as a process of learning by doing. Planning by objectives, which implies give and take, and building consensus while maintaining one's identity are key elements of these processes. As the CAMPlab experience and other projects demonstrate, the challenge is now to consolidate the new organizations and to strengthen their community roots and ties.

## Assessing practice: key factors determining success or failure

A critical review of IDRC's past investment and experience in participatory research, allow us to identify a number of factors that appear key to the success of participatory research (Found 1995; see also Vernooy 1996). Throughout this book, especially in chapters 6 and 7, we look at the CAMPlab project in the light of these factors.

One key factor is the fit or resonance of a project with local sociocultural circumstances, in terms of not only values, aspirations, and interests, but also organizational presence. If farmers or fishermen and researchers have different points of departure, i.e., relatively well-off versus poor, urban versus rural, with access to outsiders versus isolated, and if these differences are unrecognized or not understood by the researchers, the participatory process is more likely to fail. As a result, seemingly sound research tools, technologies, or organizational innovations employed or developed by projects will not be accepted or implemented by local people.

A related dimension is the need for researchers to be, as much as possible, on the same wavelength as local people. This implies that researchers must challenge their own thinking and question their assumptions ("cultural baggage") and material (class) interests. In other words, researchers have to put themselves into the shoes of local people and reflect on their motivation, attitudes, abilities, and roles (Pottier 1995; McAllister 1999). This has also been emphasized by other researchers; Bentley (1994), for example, points out that social distance between local people and researchers is a major limitation for effective participatory research.

A little-researched factor is a shared common background among the professional researchers themselves. Where a common academic or professional background exists, the participatory process will be more effective (IDRC 1988).

Another factor is the specificity of the definition of who participates and how participation takes place. The less clearly the process is defined, the more likely it will not be effective (IDRC 1988). Closely linked to the question of who participates is the degree of heterogeneity found at the local and supra-local levels. Here the question that must be asked is "How effective will stakeholder-driven approaches be in a given context?" Researchers must be aware that the participatory research process itself is part of the construction of a new reality and that, in most cases, this means that they will become enrolled in projects and alliance-making efforts of some individuals or groups (Pottier 1995). The notion that the researcher is neutral no longer holds.

The availability of sufficient time, financial resources, and labour and the dedication or commitment of stakeholders involved in the project are crucial to effective participatory research. This highlights the need to set aside funds and staff to support local-level initiatives or to accept the involvement of "outsiders."

Training of participants in how to be partners in a research and development initiative is another important factor. As a review report (IDRC 1988, p. 20) points out, "The establishment of partnerships among groups of people (researchers and community members) to carry out novel tasks may often be an assiduous undertaking." Experience shows that training should be followed by networking and that time is needed for the emergence of partnerships (Hinchcliffe et al. 1999). This requires frequent face-to-face interaction and a medium-to-long-term project timeframe. The support of a stable but dynamic organization, such as a research centre, can be of great help in the training and networking process.

Factors that lie outside the immediate scope of the project environment, such as political context (including political system, policies, legislation) and the macroeconomic situation can also have an influence (McAllister 1999). A political regime or policy environment that is suspicious of or even hostile toward grassroots movements and initiatives could severely limit a project's activities. On the other hand, implementation of decentralization policies might have a positive/enabling effect.

## Structure of this book

The following chapters present and analyze problems and possible alternatives for natural resource management processes in coastal regions, using the Pearl Lagoon case study as an example. Building on the personal experiences and research of the authors and those of a number of local collaborators, we highlight the successes and constraints of the CAMPlab initiative and some of the reasons behind them. Our experience shows that it is possible for people to develop alternative strategies despite a hostile political and policy environment.

*Chapter 2, The people and natural resources of Pearl Lagoon*, gives a detailed description of the study area. In the first part of the chapter, we briefly discuss demographics, ethnicity, and social organization; in the second part, we turn our attention to the landscape, ecological systems, and types of natural resource tenure and use. The coast is revealed as an area rich in natural and human resources, yet one where the sociopolitical context limits the potential for their sustainable management.

*Chapter 3, No life without fish: a local history of fish resources and their use*, presents the views of local people on the fish resources in the basin. Local history provides additional insight into the general character of the region and gives rise to a number of the themes that are the subjects of the following chapters. The issues addressed include the ups and downs in the fisheries sector and related changes in the relation between fishing for domestic and local use and commercial fisheries; changes in technology and their impact; the role of women; resource depletion and environmental issues; and local answers to resource use problems.

***Chapter 4, "Going far to catch a fish": local perceptions of the dynamics and impact of a changing resource base***, focuses on people's perceptions of the impact of the changes in the fisheries in three Pearl Lagoon villages (Haulover, Kakabila, and Orinoco) and the reactions that the changes have provoked among the people of these communities. This example of a largely indigenous rural population trying to deal with the effects of increasing commercialization of natural resources is common in the basin and on the Caribbean coast. It offers us an opportunity to examine the ability and desire of such communities to modify the changes, based on local norms and values, in ways that make them more equitable and sustainable in socioeconomic and environmental terms. The chapter summarizes insights obtained from the field research carried out by Mark Hostetler and communal CAMPlab investigators (Hostetler 1998).

***Chapter 5, CAMPlab: the Coastal Area Monitoring Project and Laboratory***, focuses on the organizational component of the CAMPlab research process with particular attention to the CAMPlab committees, the design and implementation of a series of environmental monitoring activities (water, forest and fish catch), the mapping and demarcation of indigenous lands project, and the ups and downs in the development of an integrated natural resource management plan for the lagoon.

***Chapter 6, Walking a fine line: the dynamics of the participatory action research process***, addresses the dynamics, strengths, and constraints of the research process. To understand the viability of the CAMPlab PAR process, one clearly needs to locate it within this complex sociopolitical context. Doing this reveals how the research process resonated or conflicted with local peoples' aspirations and social norms. This, in turn, helps to explain CAMPlab's ability to recruit and retain participants whose energy is the vital force behind the PAR process. Eventually, and as documented for larger social movements, a collective identity among PAR participants began to emerge, based on shared aspirations, goals, and experiences. This chapter, and parts of chapters 5 and 7, are based on the field research carried out by Patrick Christie (1999) in cooperation with the CAMPlab team.

***Chapter 7, Working with the people: lessons learned***, reflects on what we learned in terms of methodology, its effectiveness in empowerment and social change, capacity-building, and natural resource management; and addresses the factors that enable or constrain the use of a PAR approach. We also summarize CAMPlab's contribution to a new way of problem solving and policy making on Nicaraguan's Caribbean coast.

The CAMPlab research process draws strength from its strong resonance with participants' long-time aspirations for self-determination and sustainable use of natural resources, which are the basis of the local economy and way of life. Successes include an improved local understanding of ecosystems and relations of humans to these systems. Local people have begun to take action, among others, through water quality improvements, reforesting local savannas, deterring forest fires, engaging local and regional officials in dialogue, and designing an integrated natural resource management plan for the Pearl Lagoon basin. Organizational and innovative capacities have been strengthened.

The quantity and quality of participation could be improved by further strengthening the research capabilities and facilitation skills of core CAMPlab staff and CAMPlab committees in the communities. Among other benefits, this would allow them to reach out to a larger group of people, involve young people more actively, and balance the current unequal participation of men and women in terms of numbers and kinds of involvement in the process. Training in participatory monitoring and evaluation techniques would provide a stronger base for reflection about these and other issues pertaining to participation, including an analysis of the meaning of "community" and the gendered nature of decision-making processes.

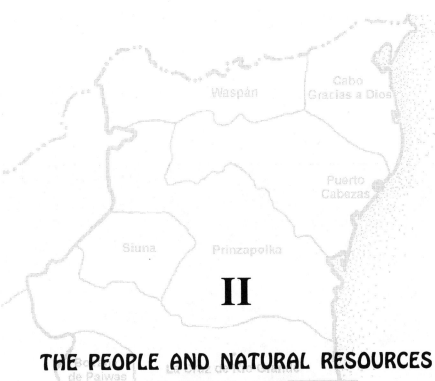

# II

# THE PEOPLE AND NATURAL RESOURCES OF PEARL LAGOON

Photo: CIDCA

# 2. THE PEOPLE AND NATURAL RESOURCES OF PEARL LAGOON

*Patrick Christie*

Although change is natural in coastal lagoons, the rate of change in parts of the Pearl Lagoon basin has recently been considerably affected by human activity. Fisheries resources are under increased pressure; new agricultural and expanded logging activities have disturbed much of the forest; and the southern and western shores of the lagoon are rapidly eroding, primarily due to wind-driven wave action that may be exacerbated by recent changes in current patterns that have resulted from dredging and deforestation of the lagoon's shoreline.

In addition to anthropogenic changes, natural catastrophes, such as Hurricane Joan in 1988, have also changed the landscape surrounding Pearl Lagoon. Large areas of forest, especially in the southern third of the lagoon, were destroyed by the hurricane. In 1998, the driest year of the decade due to effects of El Niño, fires burned large tracks of forest at the northern end of the lagoon.

However, several areas, such as parts of the lowland rainforest in western and northern portions of Pearl Lagoon's watershed, have escaped the double threat, and the basin is still considered to be one of the most pristine areas on the Caribbean coast of Central America. Nevertheless, reflections about the current dynamics of people and natural resources and future patterns seem warranted. In the first part of this chapter, we briefly discuss demographics, ethnicity, and social organization; in the second part, we turn our attention to the landscape, ecological systems, linkages between systems and system components, and types of natural resource tenure and use.

## Ethnicity and demographics

The multi-ethnicity of the coast is one of its most notable characteristics. Spanish-speaking Mestizos are now in the majority, and the indigenous Miskitu represent the second largest group. Creoles, whose language is predominantly Creole English, are descended mainly from Africans brought to work on plantations as slaves in the early 1800s (Gordon 1998). Bluefields, Corn Island, Pearl Lagoon, and, to a lesser extent, Bilwi (Puerto Cabezas) are major Creole population centres.

The Mayagna or Sumu population is spread throughout the forested areas of the northern coast, mostly in isolated communities. Some individual families live along the Escondido River south of Pearl Lagoon and in the village of Karawala at the mouth of the Río Grande of Matagalpa. The Caribs or Garifuna are African–Arawak descendants who arrived from Honduras in the late 19th century. The smallest indigenous group is the Rama who probably migrated from South America in the 18th century. They are now concentrated on a small island, Rama Cay, in Bluefields Bay, although a few Rama families can also be found in rural communities of southeast Nicaragua.

English, Spanish, and several indigenous languages are spoken on the coast (Table 1). Some Costeños speak as many as five different languages. The Miskitu, Mayagna, and Rama languages belong to the South American Macrochibcha family. The Rama language has become almost extinct; only a few, older people still speak it. (In Table 1, the Rama language is included in "Other.")

**Table 1. Population of the Southern (RAAS) and Northern (RAAN) Autonomous Atlantic Regions, 1995.**

| Language group | RAAS | RAAN | Total |
|---|---|---|---|
| Spanish | 183 186 | 94 537 | 277 723 (78%) |
| Miskitu | 3 839 | 52 380 | 56 219 (16%) |
| Mayagna | 210 | 4 297 | 4 507 (1%) |
| English | 16 546 | 1 763 | 18 309 (5%) |
| Other | 144 | 69 | 213 |
| Total | 203 925 | 153 046 | 356 971[a] (100%) |

Source: Adapted from INEC (1996, p. 106).
a. The total population in the RAAS and RAAN represents 8.2% of Nicaragua's total population, which is 4 357 099 (INEC 1996, p. 79).

Cultural relations between ethnic groups on the coast have been well researched. Miskitu domination of the region, as a result of their affiliation with the British colonists, lasted into the 19th century. By the 1880s and into the early 1900s, Creole influence reached its zenith, and this group dominated in administrative and teaching positions, especially in Bluefields and Pearl Lagoon. However, eventually, beginning with the incorporation of the coast into Nicaragua in 1894, Creole and Miskitu influence in politics, administration, and education diminished as these groups were largely displaced by the Mestizo population (Gordon 1998).

As one might expect given the colonial history of the coast, the religious profile is distinct from that of the largely Catholic interior and the Pacific coast (Table 2). Originally, German and British missionaries introduced Moravian and Anglican traditions, respectively. Catholicism arrived with Nicaraguan immigrants and foreign Catholic missionaries (e.g., Capuchins). Evangelistic denominations, such as Seventh Day Adventist, which were introduced mainly by missionaries from the United States and spread by local followers, are increasingly important both in the cities of Bluefields and Bilwi and in rural communities.

**Table 2. Religions of the people of the Southern (RAAS) and Northern (RAAN) Autonomous Atlantic Regions, 1995.**

| Religion | RAAS | RAAN | Total |
|---|---|---|---|
| Catholic | 128 148 | 71 925 | 200 073 (56%) |
| Evangelical | 37 789 | 27 496 | 65 285 (18%) |
| Moravian | 9213 | 40 703 | 49 916 (14%) |
| Episcopal | 3 345 | 290 | 3 635 (1%) |
| Other | 8 329 | 4 292 | 12 621 (4%) |
| None | 17 101 | 8 340 | 25 441 (7%) |
| Total | 203 925 | 153 046 | 356 971 (100%) |

Source: Adapted from INEC (1996, p. 112).

## The population of Pearl Lagoon

According to the 1995 census, the total population of the Pearl Lagoon communities including Pueblo Nuevo is 6253 (CIDCA-UCA 1996). Official figures for individual communities are not available; however, based on an unofficial census conducted by Acción Médica Cristiana in 1992, the lagoon's population is concentrated in four communities: the town of Pearl Lagoon, Tasbapauni, Haulover, and Orinoco (Table 3). During the 1980s when migration into the area was low, Pearl Lagoon's population grew by about 3% annually (CIDCA 1987). If we rely on the figures from the unofficial 1992 census (5209) and the 1995 government census (6253), the rate of population growth clearly increased in the 1990s to about 8% annually. This is likely a result of the arrival of colonists from the interior and the repatriation of families displaced during the war. However, these figures may not be accurate.

**Table 3. Estimated population[a] of Pearl Lagoon communities, 1992.**

| Community | Ethnicity | Men | Women | Total no. | % of total |
|---|---|---|---|---|---|
| Awas[b] | Miskitu | 47 | 38 | 85 | 1.3 |
| Brown Bank | Creole | 74 | 64 | 138 | 2.2 |
| Haulover[c] | Miskitu–Creole | 490 | 510 | 1000 | 16.0 |
| Kakabila | Miskitu | 144 | 122 | 266 | 4.3 |
| La Fe | Garifuna | 122 | 136 | 258 | 4.2 |
| Town of Pearl Lagoon | Creole | 683 | 774 | 1457 | 23.5 |
| Marshall Point | Creole | 122 | 132 | 254 | 4.0 |
| Orinoco | Garifuna | 395 | 429 | 824 | 13.3 |
| Raitipura | Miskitu | 78 | 77 | 155 | 2.5 |
| San Vicente | Garifuna | 74 | 68 | 142 | 2.3 |
| Set Net Point | Miskitu–Creole | 44 | 50 | 94 | 1.5 |
| Tasbapauni | Miskitu | 539 | 537 | 1076 | 17.3 |
| Pueblo Nuevo[d] | Mestizo | 226 | 234 | 460 | 7.4 |
| Totals | | 2548 (49%) | 2661 (51%) | 5209 | |

Source: Acción Médica Cristiana (1992 informal census).

a. Official figures are not available, and other studies have reported different population figures for these communities (e.g., White, A. [1994], reported 876 residents for Orinoco). These figures are probably underestimates.

b. Awas is a recently established community by people originally from Raitipura.

c. Haulover was excluded from the Acción Médica Cristiana study; its estimated population is based on its size relative to other communities.

d. Pueblo Nuevo is not on the lagoon, but upstream on the Wawashang River.

Pearl Lagoon communities are ethnically diverse. Raitipura, Awas, Kakabila, and Tasbapauni are mainly Miskitu. Haulover, originally a Miskitu community, has been "Creolized" to a large extent due to its proximity to the town of Pearl Lagoon, which, along with Brown Bank, Marshall Point, and Set Net, is a Creole community. Orinoco, San Vicente, and La Fe are Garifuna. Pueblo Nuevo and Wawashang are Mestizo agricultural communities in the Wawashang River basin. Although this situation is changing as people from the various communities intermarry, each town still retains a distinct ethnicity based on linguistic, economic, or cultural characteristics. According to population estimates (and if Haulover is categorized as a Creole community), Creoles are the most populous group in the Pearl Lagoon region; the population consists of 47.2% Creole, 25.4% Miskitu, 19.8% Garifuna, and 7.4% Mestizo.

## Formal and informal organizations

A diverse web of social organizations is an important feature of the lagoon. The town of Pearl Lagoon is the centre of social, political, and economic life in the basin. Both mayors of the municipality since 1990 have been from this town.

Originally, a committee of elders was the principal decision-making body in each community. During the Somoza era, an appointed government liaison official from the community (the *síndico*) became influential. Today, the most important local political organizations are the communal councils, which exist in each community, and the mayor and municipal council, who are elected. Representatives of most major organizations, such as the school, unions, churches, and sports associations, are represented on the communal council. In more traditional communities, such as Tasbapauni, tensions exist between the still extant committee of elders and the communal council.

The delineation of responsibilities of the communal and municipal councils is not well defined. Each works to encourage local development, but the mayor and the municipal council are recognized at the regional and national levels.

The mayor's office has been involved in approving timber concessions and controlling such controversial activities such as trawling for shrimp in the lagoon. Thus, the mayor's office has influence over the use of natural resources by controlling minor logging concessions, issuing building permits for fish processing plants, and collecting taxes.

Churches also play a critical role in the social lives of most people on the coast. Religious holidays and weekly days of worship are observed by most people. Churches are also involved in community development in areas such as education, health, and the environment. Moravian, Baptist, Seventh Day Adventists, and Anglican are the largest churches.

Since the mid-1980s, development agencies have played an important role in Pearl Lagoon communities, filling the void left by the lack of government services. During the early 1990s, several NGOs were very active. Until 1995, Consejo de Iglesias Evangélicas Pro-Alianza Denominación was engaged in encouraging fish marketing, agricultural development, and the construction of dry latrines. Acción Médica Cristiana, in coordination with the Ministry of Health, is involved in immunization, clean water campaigns, and medical treatment at the local health centre. Since 1988, Norwegian Popular Aid has sponsored a large fisheries development project that involves a fish processing plant, a marine laboratory in Haulover (associated with CIDCA and the CAMPlab project), and union organizing activities. Since the early 1980s, CIDCA has carried out several research projects in the area and currently coordinates the CAMPlab project. Action Aid is a large British agency that funds various communal development projects. The Foundation for Autonomy and Development of the Caribbean coast of Nicaragua is an NGO established by coastal Frente Sandinista de Liberación Nacional political activists and is involved in education, reforestation, and community development.

Since 1994, the central government has had an increased presence in Pearl Lagoon. With the assistance of the government of the Netherlands, the fisheries division within the Ministry of Economic Development (MEDE-PESCA) initiated a multimillion-dollar bilateral fisheries development project: Proyecto de Desarrollo Integral de la Pesca Artesanal en Laguna de Perlas (DIPAL). In 1997, the Ministry of Natural Resources and Environment (MARENA) opened a small local office and continues to coordinate logging concessions and forest management in the area.

## The landscape

The Pearl Lagoon area has been shaped by the geologic forces of ancient volcanoes, the rise and fall of the sea level, and meandering rivers. In general, the terrain around the lagoon is very flat with only a 7-m variation in elevation. Kukra Hill to the south of the lagoon is an ancient volcano and tertiary volcanic deposits reach the western shores of the lagoon in several places (Radley 1960). Wide expanses of alluvial deposits are broken by occasional hills of volcanic deposits. The savannas are composed of marine deposits of sand.

To the east, a thin ridge, called the Caribal Peninsula, separates the lagoon from the Caribbean Sea (see Figure 3). Radley (1960) hypothesizes that the lagoon was carved out by the Río Grande de Matagalpa and that the main rivers flowing into the lagoon today were once its tributaries. According to this theory, the resistant ancient sea deposits of compacted sand that run along the Caribal Peninsula deflected the Río Grande on this southerly course. As sea levels rose, the lower reaches of the rivers were flooded, and wind and wave action eroded and widened the lagoon.

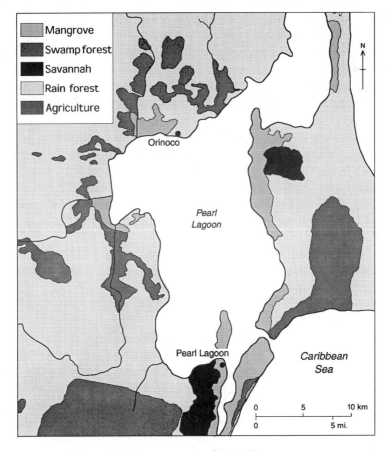

**Figure 3. Ecosystems of Pearl Lagoon.**

## Waterways

The Kurinwás, Wawashang, Patch, and Ñari rivers, in order from north to south, are the largest rivers flowing into the lagoon. The volume of fresh water they carry is so great that, during the peak of the wet season, the rivers force the saltwater out of the lagoon. In 1927, a 3-km canal was built to connect the southern portion of the lagoon with the Silico River, which allowed for boat travel to Bluefields. In the 1960s, another canal was dug to connect the northern portion of the lagoon with the Río Grande de Matagalpa. Without baseline data, the effects of these changes on the lagoon remain unclear, but they probably altered circulation and drainage patterns significantly.

**25**

The rivers provide habitat for a rich diversity of life that has yet to be studied intensively. Freshwater species such as cichlids (*Cichlasoma* spp.) and brackish water species such as tarpon (*Megalops atlantica*), especially during their juvenile stages, and snook (*Centropomus* spp.) inhabit the rivers (Robins and Ray 1986). The once-common Caiman (*Caiman crocodiles*) and crocodiles (*Crocodylus acutus*) have been heavily exploited. Freshwater shrimp (*Macrobrachium carcinus*) is a valuable, but largely uncommercialized, resource found in the rivers. Southern river otters (*Lutra longicaudus*) have been observed in the area, but their abundance is unknown.

The waterways provide the main access to farmland and hunting grounds in the interior, and the Río Grande de Matagalpa is a major route for people from the interior of Nicaragua traveling to the Caribbean coast. Settlements of recent immigrants from inland areas can be found on the shores of the Wawashang and Patch rivers. The rivers are also important transport routes. For example, most of the timber from this area is floated down the rivers in large rafts or on barges.

Rivers are used in other ways as well. One small river, Mos Mos Creek near Haulover, is used for washing clothes during the dry season and as a source of water for fish processing plants in the town of Pearl Lagoon.

## Principal ecosystems

The Pearl Lagoon basin is remarkably diverse considering its flat terrain. Lowland rainforest, savanna, and swamp forest are the principal terrestrial ecosystems. Their distribution is determined by various physical factors, including soil composition, elevation, and topography. The most obvious aquatic ecosystems are the lagoon itself and the large rivers that supply the lagoon with enormous quantities of fresh water. Mangrove forests grow along the boundaries between these terrestrial and aquatic ecosystems in some areas. Each ecosystem harbours unique and diverse flora and fauna.

### Tropical lowland rainforests

The biological diversity of the Caribbean coast's lowland tropical rainforest is impressive. Over 250 species of trees, 255 species of birds, and 60 species of butterflies have been identified — a level of biodiversity comparable to similar ecosystems in other parts of Central America (Vandermeer et al. 1990). Large predators such as jaguars (*Felis onca*), ocelots (*F. pardalis*), and mountain lions (*F. concolor*), which are among the first species to disappear from disturbed forests, are still present in the area, although their numbers are dwindling due to hunting and loss of habitat (Robinson 1991). Fifty years ago, naturalist Archie Carr (1992) described the Pearl Lagoon area as remote and covered with primary forest teaming with a wide variety of wildlife such as collared peccary (*Tayassu tajacu*), tapir (*Tapirus bairdii*), curassow

(*Crax rubra*), scarlet macaw (*Ara macao*), and giant anteaters (*Myrmecophaga tridactyla*). These are rare in the area today.

The rainforest is affected by the climate and topography. With annual rainfall ranging from 2000 to 4000 mm, the coast is one of the wettest areas of Central America. Total rainfall increases from north to south, with the highest values recorded south of Bluefields where the hills are close to the shore. During the wet season from June to August, rains flood much of the low-lying land. A dry season occurs from mid-February to early May. Greaves (1978) reported that the mean annual rainfall for Bluefields during an unspecified 14-year period was 4184 mm; May was the driest month of the year with an average of 75 mm. Mean daily temperatures range from 25.6°C in December to 27.7°C in April, with a minimum temperature of 17°C and maximum of 35°C for Bluefields.

Mean relative humidity ranges from 86.1% (April) to 92.6% (July) (Greaves 1978). The area generally benefits from at least a slight breeze all year round, with gentle winds usually from the northeast between October and January and stronger breezes from the east and southeast between February and September. A cool northern wind occurs from November to January. The hurricane season is from June to October.

Soil type plays a large role in determining the composition of plant communities within lowland rainforests. Vandermeer (1990) differentiated between the forests on alluvial plains and those on residual, agriculturally poor soils. The forests found today on the coast are generally over weathered ultisols.

The rainforests surrounding Bluefields are made up of a diverse mosaic of associated tree species that are distinct in each location (Vandermeer et al. 1990). Some of the most common trees found in 1991 [in addition to the very common pioneer, post-hurricane species *Cecropia obtusifolia* (trompet leaf, guarumo), *Croton killipianus* (algodón), and *Croton schiedeanus* (algodón)] were *Cordia bicolor* (muñeco), *Dipteryx panamensis* (ibo, almendro), *Galipea granulosa* (pata de yankee), *Rinorea* sp. (huesito), *Dendropanax arboreus* (concha de cangrejo), *Miconia* spp. (capirote), *Pentaclethra macroloba* (gavilá), *Brosimum guianense* (ojoche blanco), *Qualea* sp. (areñón), *Hirtella americana* (guaviluno), and *Ficus popenoei* (fig tree, chilamate).

Natural disturbances play a fundamental role in the ecology of these forests. In the Pearl Lagoon area, three hurricanes in the 20th century (one in 1906, Hurricane Joan in 1988, and Hurricane Cesar in 1996) have significantly affected large areas of forest. Hurricane Joan leveled approximately 500 000 ha of forest surrounding Bluefields in October 1988. Although recent data indicate that the forest is regenerating rapidly as fallen trees resprout (Vandermeer and Perfecto 1991; Mallona 1992; Vandermeer et al. 1996), it will probably be decades before the affected area can supply timber at the pre-hurricane level. Although the ecological role of such

**27**

natural disturbances is unclear, such events are likely an important force contributing to the high biodiversity of tropical rainforests on the coast (Connell 1978; Vandermeer et al. 1996).

### Pine savannas

Although the importance of the rainforest has been well documented, pine savanna is of equal value for some Pearl Lagoon communities. The area contains the southernmost natural extension of *Pinus caribaea* var. *hondurensis* and its associated ecosystem, the pine savanna. From the Nicaragua–Honduras border to the canal between Pearl Lagoon and Bluefields Bay, pine-dominated systems cover approximately 453 000 (IRENA 1990) of the approximately 1 million ha of savanna along the Caribbean coast.

The soils of this ecosystem are a mixture of red-yellow latosols in better drained areas and hydromorphic soils in low-lying areas (Taylor 1962; Greaves 1978). The silicious sand and gravel soils are the result of deposits made as the sea level rose and fell during the Pliocene and Pleistocene (Parsons 1955; Radley 1960; Greaves 1978). Below a thin layer of these sandy soils is an impervious subsoil with iron concretions that limits the passage of water, thus creating large flooded areas during the wet season (Parsons 1955). The soils are slightly acidic (pH 5–6). The amount of organic matter and nitrogen they contain is low, greatly limiting their use for agriculture.

Two distinct plant communities occur in the savanna: open sedge savanna and pine–oak–nance savanna. Above the flood level during the rainy season, one finds Caribbean pine and stunted pyrophytic trees, such as sandpaper tree (*Curatella americana*), oak (*Quercus oleoides*), and nance (*Byrsonima crassifolia*), as well as brush (Melastomaceae and Myrtaceae) and thickly growing grasses and sedges. Clewell (1986) reports 28 species of plants in the pine–oak–nance ecosystem, with grasses more common than sedges.

Below the flood level, one finds primarily grasses, sedges, and clumps of palmetto (*Acoelorrhaphe wrightii*). Clewell (1986) reports 165 species of plants in this system, with an overlap of 22 species (13%) with northwest Florida. Sedges are more common than grasses in this system. In areas where water persists, hydromorphic soils are found. A widespread algae crust is indicative of areas that are flooded much of the year (Greaves 1978).

Plants that are considered typical pioneer rainforest species (e.g., *Croton smithianus*, *Cecropia obtusifolia*, and *Isertia hankeana*) as well as coppice varieties (*Davilla kunthii* and *Q. oleoides*), are found in dense thickets (or "keys" as they are called locally) scattered throughout the generally open savanna. These thickets do not usually burn, possibly due to elevated moisture levels in these areas.

As with the rainforests, human actions are a critical component of the natural history of pine savannas, and fires and logging have had a significant impact. The sandy soils and vegetation of the savanna dry quickly during the brief, but intense, dry season, allowing fires to spread rapidly. Estimates of the frequency of burning in most savanna areas without fire suppression programs vary from almost annually (Taylor 1962) to once every 3 (Greaves 1978) to 5 years (Clewell 1986). In the southern Pearl Lagoon area, the frequency of burning for any given area varies from 3 to 5 years, depending on the particular use and its proximity to human traffic. Most burning is done to encourage new growth of grass for cattle and deer, to uncover animal burrows (i.e., turtles and iguanas), to kill pests, and for amusement, although some fires are caused by lightening.

Today, only a small fragment of the original pine forest of southern Pearl Lagoon remains. It lies approximately 0.5 km southwest of Haulover and is known locally as the Fine Pine Wood. This stand of trees is used as a gathering place for church picnics during the Easter season, which is probably why local residents have preserved it. Pine savanna also extends from west of the town of Pearl Lagoon across the Moncada Canal to an area called Pinal. These areas have been significantly affected by logging, fires, and Hurricane Joan. A third savanna, named Pine Ridge, is located on the Caribal Peninsula. It contains mature trees, but is currently being logged by small-scale loggers, and no attempts at reforestation are being made.

Although the Miskitu do not use the savanna for subsistence needs any more than other coastal ecosystems (Nietschmann 1973), the towns of Pearl Lagoon and Haulover rely on it for extensive cattle rearing, deer and armadillo (*Dasypus novemcinctus*) hunting, and small-scale timber and firewood extraction. Past extraction and disturbances have degraded the savannas to the point where most people regard them as mismanaged wastelands.

### Swamp forests

Swamp forests cover vast expanses of the low areas of the coast. Swamps have been reported to cover 107 900 ha in the RAAS (Robinson 1991), but this is likely an underestimate. Urquhart (1997) estimates that Hurricane Joan severely damaged approximately 100 000 ha of swamp forest; 90 000 ha of this forest burned the following year, killing most of the trees. Herbaceous vegetation, such as the pioneering fern (*Blechnum serrulatum*), or a mat of grass came to dominate this system after the hurricane, probably a temporary situation as *B. serrulatum* is shade intolerant. The presence of charcoal layers and *B. serrulatum* spores in Urquhart's (1997) soil cores indicates that burning is a recurring event in these swamps.

In lower, wetter areas, palms such as *Raphia taedigera* become the dominant vegetation and may cover extensive areas of swamp. *R. taedigera*-dominated swamps may eventually become filled with organic matter and alluvium, resulting in soil conditions that will allow the establishment of hardwood species (Vandermeer 1991).

In areas with less standing water, hardwood species such as *Pterocarpus officianalis* (sangredrago), *Calophyllum brasiliense* (sabba, santa maría), *Vochysia guatemalensis* (palo de agua), and *Symphonia globulifera* (leche maría) are common. Less common tree species are *Terminalia oblonga* (guayabán), *Carapa guianensis* (cedro macho), *Dipteryx panamensis* (ibo, almendro), *Pentaclethra macroloba* (gavilán), and *Prioria copaifera* (cativo) (Vandermeer 1991; Urquhart 1997).

The swamp forest is used in a variety of ways by the people of Pearl Lagoon. Rice production is common in swamps. Logging of such valuable hardwood species as *Calophyllum brasiliense*, *Carapa guianensis*, and *Symphonia globulifera*, has also reduced their numbers in many swamp forests (Urquhart 1997). Local people maintain that most of the swamp forest in the Pearl Lagoon basin has already been logged. Hunting is also an important practice, especially for the Miskitu; preferred game are deer and white-lipped peccary, but paca (*Cuniculus paca*) and agouti (*Dasyprocta punctata*) are also hunted.

## Mangrove forests

Mangrove forests occur between terrestrial and aquatic systems. Mangroves cover 60 000 ha of Nicaragua's Caribbean coast, with about 26 000 ha in the RAAS (Robinson 1991; García and Camacho 1994). The most common species, occurring in order from open water to drier ground are red mangrove (*Rhizophora mangle*), black mangrove (*Avicennia germinans*), and white mangrove (*Languncularia racemosa*). Also present are the buttonwood mangrove (*Conocarpus erectus*) and tea mangrove (*Pelliceria rhizophorae*), a species that until recently had only been reported on the Pacific coast of Central America (Roth and Grijalva 1991).

In Pearl Lagoon, mangroves cover a large portion of the eastern shoreline, although the exact extent is unknown. Except in the southern part of the lagoon, which was heavily affected by Hurricane Joan and harvesting, the mangroves appear to be mature, some reaching a height of over 25 m. Disturbed areas are covered with such herbaceous plants as the fern *B. serrulatum* (Guilfoyle 1994).

Mangroves play several important ecological roles. For example, they create a habitat for a variety of valuable fish and shrimp species. They also serve as natural barriers to waves and protect shorelines from erosion and inundation during storms. The presence of mangroves probably mitigated the full effect of Hurricane Joan on the towns of Pearl Lagoon and Haulover.

In Haulover, 98% of the households report that they regularly use mangroves (Guilfoyle 1994). The durability of posts made of mangrove wood is well known among local people. The bark is used for tannins, and the wood makes excellent firewood. Although charcoal production from mangrove wood is common elsewhere, it is not a widespread practice in the Pearl Lagoon area. Robinson (1991) has recommended a timber extraction model for the Pearl Lagoon mangroves based on a 24-year rotation cycle that would prohibit cutting along the shores of the lagoon and rivers. Guilfoyle (1994) recommended complete closure of some harvested areas in Pearl Lagoon for 30 years.

Indirect products of mangrove forests are also important to local communities. The role of mangroves as nurseries for fish and shellfish is probably the most important indirect benefit. White shrimp (*Penaeus schmitti*), snook (*Centropomus* spp.), snapper (*Lutjanus* spp.), whitemouth croaker (*Micropogon furnieri*), and seacats (*Bagre marinus*) are only some of the important commercial species that use mangrove areas at some stage of their life cycle. Recently, commercial fishing for crab (*Callinectes sapidus* and *C. bocourti*), which depend on the mangroves, has begun.

Mangrove forests are not used for mariculture to any degree in Pearl Lagoon, although central government officials view this as an important industry to develop. Without due consideration of the critical ecological role that mangroves play, shrimp mariculture, on the scale at which it is practised in Southeast Asia, Ecuador, and the Pacific coast of Nicaragua, would probably have serious consequences for local artisanal fishers (Suman 1994; Hopkins et al. 1995). In addition to the negative effects of mangrove deforestation, large-scale operations might also result in overexploitation of shrimp larvae populations, overuse of freshwater sources, and contamination of the lagoon with excess nutrients.

### The lagoon

Pearl Lagoon is a large expanse of brackish water fed by four main rivers and various smaller creeks with a 200-m wide opening into the Caribbean Sea (Fig. 1). The area of Pearl Lagoon is approximately 52 000 ha, making it the largest coastal lagoon on Nicaragua's Caribbean coast. The lagoon is shallow — from 0.5 to 12 m deep. The salinity of the lagoon varies seasonally and spatially from almost fresh water to concentrations of 34 parts salt per thousand of water (ppt) (CAMPlab unpublished data; DIPAL 1996a). Salinity decreases with distance from the opening to the sea, but depends largely on tidal intake of seawater and the amount of fresh water entering the lagoon from the rivers.

The substrate of the lagoon is mostly mud and sand, although there are some rocky areas and large oyster (*Crassostrea* sp.) reefs mainly near the opening to the Caribbean sea. The level of dissolved oxygen ranges from 3 to 8 mg/L. In 1995, the lowest levels were found in Big Bay (3.0 mg/L) in November and the highest level (7.8 mg/L) near Brown Bank in June (CAMPlab, unpublished data; DIPAL 1996a).

In the northern section of the lagoon, temperatures can range from 25°C in November and December to 33°C between May and September. pH varies from 6 to 7.5. The lagoon is generally turbid: Secchi disk measurements range from 0.3 to 1.8 m, with turbidity increasing during the wet season as rivers bring sediments from the surrounding region, likely the system's most important source of nutrients.

According to Kjerfve and Magill's (1989) classification system, Pearl Lagoon is most appropriately described as a "choked system," meaning that the opening to the ocean is limited. The lagoon exhibits little tidal variation and the turnover time of its waters is long. It is likely that Pearl Lagoon is well mixed vertically, given its shallow depth and the constant winds of the coast; however, it exhibits considerable horizontal stratification of salinity. During heavy rains, extensive flooding of adjacent lands is not uncommon because of the restricted opening to the ocean.


**The fish population**

To date, 46 species of fish have been identified in the lagoon, although this figure does not include a number of noncommercial species. Tropical estuaries are generally considered to be places of high nekton biomass but low species diversity compared with other tropical marine and freshwater systems (McKlusky 1981; Day et al. 1989). The true ichthyofaunal diversity is likely to be somewhere between the 67 species identified in Tortuguero Estuary, Costa Rica (Stoner 1986, citing Gilbert and Kelso 1971) and the 121 species identified by Yañez-Arancibia et al. (1980) in Terminos Lagoon, Mexico.

As is common in coastal lagoons, a few species are clearly the most common, especially catfish *(Bagre marinus)* (CAMPlab unpublished data; DIPAL 1996b). Some of the most important commercial species are snook (*Centropomus* spp.), snapper (*Lutjanus* spp.), stripped mojarra (*Eugerres plumieri, Gerres cinereus*), catfish (*Bagre marinus*), whitemouth croaker (*Micropogonius furnieri*), mackerel (*Scomberomorus brasiliensis*), crevalle jack (*Caranx hippos*), and coppermouth (*Cynoscion* spp.). At least five commercially important shrimp species have been found in the lagoon and near the shore: brown shrimp (*Penaeus aztecus*), white shrimp (*P. schmitti*), pink shrimp (*P. duorarum, P. brasiliensis*), and Atlantic seabob (*Xiphopenaeus kroyeri*).

The distribution of fish and shrimp in the lagoon varies with the salinity of the lagoon. During the wet season, as the torrential rains flush the salt water out into the sea, freshwater fish such as cichlids and brackish water fish such as snook (*Centropomus parallelus* and *C. pectinatus*) move from the rivers into the lagoon. The abundance of fish in the lagoon during the rainy season is likely to be at least partly the result of the high input of allochthonous detritus and associated food (Stoner 1986). Meanwhile, white shrimp that have been growing through their juvenile stages in the lagoon are driven out into the ocean where they reproduce.

During the dry season, the salinity rises and saltwater-intolerant fish move back into the rivers, while large schools of seafish (e.g., jack) move into the lagoon and Atlantic seabob shrimp reach the lagoon's opening. Not all species are able to tolerate this dynamic environment, although some (e.g., *Bagre marinus*, *Centropomus undecimalis*, *Micropogonias furnieri*, *Eugerrres plumieri*) are found in the lagoon all year long. McClusky (1981) maintains that fish species move into this ecosystem to exploit rich food supplies, to avoid predation, and to take advantage of the low level of interspecific competition.

Fish distribution is also influenced by substrate and vegetation. Mud bottoms and patches of *Rupia* spp. and *Halodule* were generally found to be the preferred areas for fish and shrimp in lagoons along the coast (Marshall et al. 1995). Local residents report that juvenile shrimp use the seagrass beds for refuge. Mangrove prop roots also provide an important habitat for fish and shrimp (Day et al. 1989; Marshall et al. 1995).

The lagoon plays an important role in maintaining fish populations, both resident species and those that spend the majority of their life cycle in the sea. Reproduction of many of the fish (e.g., whitemouth croaker, snook, and *Bardiella rhonchus*) is partial or asynchronic, meaning that spawning typically happens more than once during the year rather than in a well-defined spawning period (Isaac 1988; DIPAL 1996b). Top-Lock Lagoon to the north and the canal to the south are reported by local fishers to be important nursery grounds for snook and other species.

According to ecological studies (Volpe 1959; Thue et al. 1982; Rutherford et al. 1986; Tucker and Campbell 1988; McMichael et al. 1989; DIPAL 1996b) confirmed by interviews of local fishers (CAMPlab unpublished data), it is likely that *Centropomus undecimalis*, a snook species, reproduces mainly just outside the lagoon's opening to the ocean. Peak spawning probably occurs during the new moon from March to June (when water temperatures are 30–31°C). One study reported that once *C. undecimalis* are 457 mm in length, or 2–3 years old, approximately half are mature (Rutherford et al. 1986). Other genera of fish, such as tarpon, snapper, and croaker, are likely to spawn offshore, with their juveniles using the lagoon as a nursery (Rutherford et al. 1986).

The lagoon is also the habitat for a number of threatened species, such as crocodile and manatee (*Trichechus manatus*). These species continue to be hunted for their skin and meat, respectively, by local people (Nickerson 1995). The manatee are particularly vulnerable to harpooning during the dry season, when phosphorescent plankton reveal their location and movement at night.

## Recent changes in the lagoon

In the recent past, physical aspects of the lagoon have been considerably altered. In addition to connecting the lagoon with other waterways, a deepwater passage through the lagoon was dredged to facilitate boat travel. Local fishers have indicated that large areas of oyster reef and trees have been killed in the swamps where the dredges deposited the sediments they removed. Natural islands created from dredged sediments are scattered throughout the southern portion of the lagoon. The unnatural waste-islands have probably contributed to changes in the lagoon's circulation and possibly to the observed patterns of shore erosion near Raitipura.

The lagoon is an area of high productivity due to the inflow of nutrient-rich waters from the highlands. However, recent changes in land use and the resulting increase in sedimentation rates in the lagoon may threaten this ecosystem. Increased sedimentation has been identified by local people and scientists as one of the environmental issues of primary importance in Pearl Lagoon (Robinson 1991; Ryan 1992; Marshall et al. 1995). If the turbidity of the lagoon increases, the more sensitive species (e.g., oysters) may be affected.

Especially important is the negative response of phytoplankton whose ability to photosynthesize will be reduced. This will lower the level of oxygen they produce by photosynthesis and, thus, decrease the amount of dissolved oxygen available to other organisms. As suspended solids absorb sunlight, the water temperature may also rise, again lowering oxygen levels in the water.

The lagoon also receives a variety of wastes originating from the human settlements on its shores. Human fecal waste from the communities surrounding Pearl Lagoon was once a problem according to local accounts, although, in recent years, the increased number of pit and dry latrines has reduced this environmental hazard. Fecal coliform tests at Haulover show 24 colonies/100 mL, well below the recommended 200 colonies/100 mL threshold for safe contact.

Despite local concerns, fish waste from at least one processing plant are reportedly being dumped into the lagoon. The discharge of oxygen-demanding organic material may result in decreased dissolved oxygen levels in the immediate area. This in turn may kill fish and affect shrimp distribution if the oxygen level drops below that required for survival (Caddy 1989; Peterson and Gilmore 1991). Such physical changes in the environment may lead to changes in the types of fish found in the lagoon, perhaps increasing the number of less commercially desirable species (Kapetsky and Lasserre 1984). On the other hand, discharges of small amounts of waste may raise the lagoon's overall productivity. Regardless of the impact, such actions set a dangerous precedence that may result in future, more serious environmental problems.

## Land and sea tenure

Land tenure on the coast is complex and confusing. The international struggle over the area and its natural resources resulted in contradictory claims by Britain and Nicaragua. In 1847, an agreement between the representative of the Nicaraguan State and Miskitu Princess Agnes Anne Frederic allowed for safe passage along the coast and claimed the coast as a Nicaraguan department. This agreement was superseded with the signing of the Managua Treaty in 1860 between Britain and Nicaragua, whereby the British renounced its claim to the coast yet established a "Mosquito Reserve" to be governed by indigenous leaders.

The creation of the reserve was clearly a means of maintaining informal British ties to the coast. In 1894, it was annexed by the Zelaya government and incorporated into the national territory as the Department of Zelaya. Finally, in 1905, the British and Nicaraguan governments signed the Harrison-Altamirano Treaty establishing the land rights of indigenous and Creole communities. Each family was to receive at least 8 manzanas (approximately 5.7 ha) of land. Eventually this scheme was deemed unworkable by British officials and the British authorities helped communities obtain communal titles beginning in 1916.

Confusion exists because claims under different communal titles overlap, descriptions of borders are based on impermanent or imprecise landmarks, and many of the titles have been misplaced. Currently, efforts are underway at the regional level with international assistance to clarify the situation (CACRC 1996, 1998). Based on one organization's documentation of land titles, approximately 18 536 ha of land surrounding Pearl Lagoon are communally owned (IPADE 1995, see Table 4). Titles were assigned to certain communities within Pearl Lagoon as a result of British allotments in 1916–1917 and the subsequent securing of supplementary communal titles. Marshall Point, Orinoco, San Vicente, La Fe, Brown Bank, and Set Net do not hold formal titles according to the same documentation. However, informal agreements between local leaders allowed these communities to be established and to have access to arable land.

## Table 4. Communal land in Pearl Lagoon communities.[a]

| Owner | Year of acquisition | Area (ha) |
|---|---|---|
| Creoles of the town of Pearl Lagoon | 1916 | 2999 |
| Miskitu and Creoles of Haulover and Raitipura | 1917 | 2076[a] |
| Miskitu of Kakabila[b] | 1917 | 1007 |
| Indigenous people of Pearl Lagoon[c] | 1941 | 6000 (beach lands) |
| People of Tasbapauni[b,d] | 1917 | 1000 |
| People of Tasbapauni[b,d] | 1917 | 1054 |
| Miskitu of Tasbapauni | 1920 | 800 |
| Miskitu of Tasbapauni | 1929 | 600 |
| Miskitu of Tasbapauni | 1960 | Unrecorded (King Cay) |
| Miskitu of Tasbapauni | 1960 | Unrecorded (Sabanok Cay) |
| Miskitu of Tasbapauni | 1957 | 3000 |
| Subtotal for Tasbapauni | | Over 6454 |
| Total communal lands in Pearl Lagoon communities | | Over 18 536 |

Source: IPADE 1995.

a. In the published collection of titles (IPADE 1995) multiple titles appeared for the same lands; only the most recent version was included.

b. Unknown subunits of hectares: "áreas" and "centiáreas" were ignored in these cases.

c. The beach lands for the indigenous people of Pearl Lagoon was reported as 20 ´ 3 ´ 20 km, likely a misprint. This was calculated as 20 ´ 3 km or 6000 ha.

d. "Creoles of Tasbapauni" then "Indigenous of Tasbapauni" were identified as the holders of different versions of titles for the same land; therefore, the generic term "People of Tasbapauni" was used.

The rules defining agricultural use of land are the clearest and most thoroughly documented. On communal lands, families have exclusive rights to the land or "plantation" that they work (Howard 1993; Jamieson 1995). Usufruct rights for a particular family or individual continue as long as they family works the parcel of land or maintains it in fallow. After years of abandonment, a parcel returns to the status of "bush" and becomes available to other communal members. The planting of perennial crops such as fruit trees, or "property" as it is referred to locally, is an important means of claiming rights to a particular parcel of land. Although the "property" on a plot of land may be sold, the land itself cannot.

Other areas are less clearly defined. Individuals from any of the Pearl Lagoon communities will hunt on other communities' communal lands, and it is not clear whether they must secure permission or be accompanied by a community member to gain access. Logging rights are similarly confusing. The level of official involved in approving any logging activity is most likely based on the scale of the activity as well as the vigilance of a community in asserting its own control over forest resources. Some communities, such as Tasbapauni, have reportedly allowed logging on their lands on payment of a "tax" to their community.

Although some communities surrounding Pearl Lagoon have legal documents demarcating their land, their rights are not always respected. Communal lands that are not being used for agriculture use are increasingly susceptible to encroachment by immigrants to the area. In the agricultural areas used by Pearl Lagoon residents (such as Rocky Point, Manhattan, Patch River, and Wawashang River), conflicts between newcomers and community members are increasingly common (see for a more detailed discussion, Chapter 4).

The concept of sea tenure does not exist in the strict sense in Pearl Lagoon. Each community has its preferred fishing grounds, but many of the most popular sites are used by a number of communities. Some residents of Tasbapauni claim exclusive rights to the northern sections of Pearl Lagoon, but increasing numbers of fishers from outside Tasbapauni are ignoring these claims. As we will discuss in Chapter 4, the communities of Pearl Lagoon do, however, collectively maintain an informal sense of sea tenure regarding "outsiders." They have, for example, successfully prevented people from Bluefields from harvesting mangrove bark.

## Resource use

### Fisheries

Although conflicting data make it difficult to gain a detailed understanding of fish and crustacean fishery production and sales, overall trends seem consistent (Martinez 1993; Ehrhardt et al. 1995; ECLAC 1996, 1997; FAO 1998). Fish harvests decreased in the 1980s allowing fish stocks to grow, but have now risen again to prewar levels. The coast supplies most of Nicaragua's shrimp (*Penaeus* spp.) and spiny lobster (*Panulirus argus*) — the shrimp harvest is two to four times that of the Pacific coast — although the catch is still significantly below prewar levels.

During the early and mid-1980s, the number of commercial trawlers significantly declined, but by the end of the decade and into the 1990s, it increased again, especially in terms of the number of foreign-owned boats. In fact, between 1988 and 1992, the percentage of shrimp caught by the national fleet was only 30–40% of the total harvest (Sánchez and Cadima 1993).

One of the most useful indices of shrimp abundance, catch-per-unit-effort (CPUE), was high for commercial boats from the late 1980s into the 1990s as the stock had not been fished heavily during the war. CPUE is leveling off or declining as fishing increases to late 1970s levels. Some analysts believe they are already seeing signs of overharvest (Ryan 1992, 1995a). This is likely, given the degree of illegal, unrecorded fishing by foreign shrimp and lobster fishing operations on the coast (Cyens 1992, Ryan 1995a). Militant Costeños, who are tired of government complacency or suspected complicity with illegal fishing, have taken matters into their own hands, some going as far as sinking an illegal shrimp trawler with a rocket-propelled grenade launcher (Cyens 1992).

The policy of relying on the Ministry of Economic Development to both develop and regulate the fisheries sector has been criticized. The ministry's dual role may result in unsustainable harvests, especially as annual revenues are partly derived from tariffs on fishing vessels (Ryan 1995a; Elizondo 1997).

The vast majority of coastal fishers are artisanal, usually with a small low-powered boat. Ryan (1995a) estimated that approximately 3000 artisanal fishers supply about 70% of the fish catch on the coast. Tensions are mounting between the artisanal fisheries sector and the central government. To the artisanal fishers, the central government seems to be on the side of the industrial, and largely foreign, fleet. The government is interested in large catches and the highest valued products for export to raise hard currency. Tension is also growing between artisanal and industrial fishing interests, especially over shrimp stocks that occupy both inshore and offshore habitats over their lifespan.

One study estimates that, in Pearl Lagoon, up to 1600 people are at least part-time fishers and that this number increases significantly when shrimp are present in the lagoon (Van der Hoeven et al. 1996). However, many of these fishers also engage in other activities, such as farming and hunting, depending on the season and the availability of fish and shrimp. In one 4-month period, although 520 different fishers sold their catch to the largest fish processor, only 35 of them had fish for sale more than once a week (Van der Hoeven et al. 1996). A related study concluded that there are only approximately 100 full-time fishers in the Pearl Lagoon area (Bouwsma et al. 1997).

The most common boat used for fishing in the lagoon is a dugout canoe, operated with paddle and sail; in 1997, 316 such vessels of various sizes operated in Pearl Lagoon (Bouwsma et al. 1997). Increasingly, successful fishers, especially those working in the sea, are using fibreglass boats, or "pangas," that are powered with outboard motors. In 1997, there were 19 pangas in Pearl Lagoon (Bouwsma et al. 1997).

Until about the 1960s, Pearl Lagoon fishers usually used hooks-and-lines and harpoons to strike fish in shallows; a practice that was only effective when fish stocks were abundant. Monofilament and multifilament gill nets, the majority of which have a 10-cm mesh, have now become the gear of choice, especially during the wet season when fish are unable to avoid the nets due to increased water turbidity (Bouwsma et al. 1997). Gill nets are deployed as either passive traps that remain stationary or are used to "circle the oyster," an operation in which a group of fishers encloses schools of fish among the oyster reefs in the lagoon.

Although gill nets seem to have been introduced in the 1960s, they remained relatively scarce until the late 1980s when government and foreign-funded development programs supplied them to fishers (see also Chapter 3). By the 1990s, they had become the most common gear. DIPAL's leasing program established contractual agreements between fishers and private fish buyers whereby, in exchange for nets, fishers extended exclusive purchase rights to the buyers until the nets were repaid. Although it is difficult to estimate the actual number of gill nets acquired, this "leasing" program spent USD 150 000 in 1994–95 to work with 28 fishers in Pearl Lagoon (Van der Hoeven et al. 1995). The recent introduction of fine-mesh nets (3" and smaller) by commercial interests has been very controversial among fishers as these nets trap numerous juvenile fish. In addition to gill nets, seine nets are also used along the beaches.

Shrimp are generally caught with cast nets and small trawls. These nets are deployed by pairs of fishers working from dories along the lagoon's shoreline and Bar Mouth where the lagoon opens into the sea. These nets are laboriously hand-woven with filaments from scraps of nylon rope; 437 of them were found in the lagoon area (Bouwsma et al. 1997). Trawl nets have been used by a few diesel boat operators from the local communities for at least the last couple of decades, but mainly for seabob shrimp (*Xiphopenaeus kroyeri*) in the Bar Mouth and out into sea. In 1997, nine such boats operated in Pearl Lagoon (Bouwsma et al. 1997).

Trawl nets were informally banned from the lagoon. In 1994, U.S. shrimp buyers introduced small trawl nets to be used by local panga owners to catch seabob as well as other Penaeid shrimp. By 1995, these fishers were ignoring the informal ban on trawling in the lagoon and were fishing among the cast-net fishers. Because of their greater efficiency and tendency to disturb the bottom of the lagoon, these trawlers are reportedly reducing the catch of cast-net fishers, who complained to local authorities. The authorities responded by sporadically preventing the trawlers from operating inside the lagoon.

The market for fish has been irregular in Pearl Lagoon. In the early 1990s, the only large-scale commercial fish-buying operations were a roaming ice boat and a cooperative fish plant in Pearl Lagoon. By 1994, two additional private operations had been established. Today, the Mar Caribe company, an operation owned by a local entrepreneur, remains the main buyer of fish and shellfish. Records of the amount of fish purchased by commercial operations give a clear indication of the rapid pace of development (Table 5).

**Table 5. Sales of major catches (kg) in the Pearl Lagoon area, 1995–97.**

| Species | 1995 | 1996 | 1997 |
|---|---|---|---|
| Shrimp (*Penaeus* spp.) | 54 316 | 25 460 | 85 191 |
| Seabob (*X. kroyeri*) | 229 739 | 164 736 | 250 793 |
| Snook (*Centropomus* spp.) | 125 958 | 182 942 | 182 890 |
| Catfish (*Bagre marinus*) | 51 692 | 64 097 | 76 178 |
| Total catch purchased, above species | 461 705 | 437 235 | 595 052 |
| Total catch purchased, all commercial species[a] | 515 087 | 563 952 | 764 002 |

Source: Adapted from Van Anrooy et al. (1998, p. 18-20).
a. Total production includes 26 species of fish and crustaceans.

In 1991, it was estimated that two-thirds of all families in Tasbapauni, Pearl Lagoon town, and Orinoco derived income from the fisheries (Gordon 1991). Although accurate estimates are not available, the recent establishment of stable commercial outlets for fish sales has encouraged increasing numbers of people in the area to become involved in the fishing industry.

Although the full implications of this shift in resource use are unclear, it is likely to have two immediate effects: increased fishing pressure in the lagoon and a shift away from agricultural activities (see for a more detailed discussion, Chapter 4).

Without proactive management of fishing activities, history tells us that the former will likely result in overexploitation of the fishery (Hilborn and Walters 1992; Cicin-Sain and Knecht 1998). The implications of the abandonment of agricultural land are less clear; the result may be regrowth of the forest. Alternatively, if immigrants move in to occupy the abandoned land, labour-intensive agroforestry systems may be replaced by less sustainable farming methods.

Pearl Lagoon is clearly entering another phase of articulation with the global economy, which implies a sharp increase in access to cash for some people. Studies estimate that the total amount of cash paid to fishers in Pearl Lagoon for their catch was USD 507 000 in 1995 and USD 1 419 000 in 1996 (Bouwsma et al. 1997, Van der Hoeven et al. 1995). These revenues have a multiplier effect on a number of businesses in the local communities. Additionally, economic growth brings associated dependence on purchased goods and foodstuffs, a situation noted by Nietschmann (1972, 1973) in the turtle fishery in the 1970s. Increasingly, generalist farmer-fishers are becoming specialist fishers who purchase their food.

Another implication of these changes is that small-scale seafood buyers and processors will increasingly become wage earners for privately-owned purchasing centres instead of entrepreneurs. For example, this has reduced opportunities for women in the communities to independently process and sell seabob. Until recently, women often either purchased wet seabob or "borrowed" seabob from their husbands and extended family and processed them into a dried, salted product with the help of family members. They sold these shrimp to itinerant buyers from Managua and Costa Rica or traveled themselves to look for markets. After selling the shrimp, which sometimes took weeks, they repaid the person who had given them the fresh shrimp.

The profit from this activity was so significant that it was referred to locally as the "lottery." In the Pearl Lagoon communities, it was an important source of capital that women controlled, and was typically used for one-time purchases of clothing or education expenses. Today, increasing numbers of fishers are selling their catch directly to Mar Caribe, the main seafood-processing plant in the area, as they are paid immediately in cash. The incentive to receive immediate payment is apparently considerable, as the amount is comparable to what they received in the original scheme.

About 30 Haulover women, some of who formerly processed seabob, are now working at Mar Caribe for approximately USD 6 per 10-h workday. Many women complain of the working conditions (especially those working in the refrigerated crab-processing centre) and the lack of a collective bargaining mechanism. The rate of turnover of employees is considerable. On the other hand, the work is available year round, as long as fish or shrimp are being caught.

The change in the type of fishing gear used also has gender implications. In Garifuna communities such as Orinoco and, to a lesser degree, in Miskitu communities such as Kakabila, women participate in the hook and line fishery (Gordon 1991; White, N. 1993; Jamieson 1995). With the large-scale introduction of the more efficient gill nets, which women generally do not use, women are fishing less frequently (as we will see in more detail in Chapter 4). In 1991, 60% of the fishers in Orinoco were women (Gordon 1991); this proportion has declined significantly and the hypothesis is that it will continue to decline as the fishery modernizes.

The potential effects of large development projects, each with their particular ideological orientations, should not be underestimated. In the 1980s, development projects that relied on labour union funds from Europe (e.g., channeled through APN), promoted the benefits of cooperative organizing and worker-owned means of production. The wartime environment of the 1980s, inexperience in managing such operations, and the unfavourable political climate of the 1990s have hindered these activities. In contrast, the new, privately-owned operations, which are receiving considerable aid through the DIPAL bilateral development program, are a fiscal success story. The combined effects of these two initiatives delivered the message that collective action is inefficient and doomed to failure.

### Agriculture

Agricultural lands are a significant component of the lagoon region. Historically, sugarcane was planted by a French settler for rum production and bananas were planted on alluvial soils. The banana and sugar plantations, which were owned by foreign entrepreneurs, replaced large areas of lowland tropical forest throughout the coast in the 19th and early 20th centuries. In the Pearl Lagoon watershed, sugarcane and banana plantations were established by both foreign and local enterprises, such as the United Fruit Company, Samuel Pondler & Co., and the Brautigam-Tom Company (Vernooy 2000).

Today, the principal forms of agriculture are small scale: beach-ridge farming, swamp rice production, swidden agriculture, agroforestry intercropping, cattle ranching, and home gardens, although to the south, large-scale sugar and oil palm (*Elaeis guineensis*) plantations still exist. Beach-ridge farming consists of the planting of coconut trees along beaches, crops such as bananas, sugarcane, and plantains on sandy ridges, and dasheen and rice in lower, wet areas. Swamp rice is planted in large areas of *Raphia* swamps. Swidden agriculture is widely practised throughout the rainforest areas. An area of land is cleared, burned, and planted, usually with corn, common beans, and various tubers. In Rocky Point the interplanting of perennials, such as coconut, cocoa, citrus fruits, pineapple, peach palm, and mango, among annual crops is common. Home gardens containing vegetables, fruits, and medicinal herbs are increasingly common throughout the Pearl Lagoon area, partly due to the assistance of development agencies interested in health issues. Cattle ranching is also common in the savannas, where cattle are allowed to roam freely.

The crops tend to be slightly different for each community, perhaps in relation to the communities' ethnicity and soil types. For example, Miskitu communities plant mostly root crops as a starch source. Both men and women are involved in farming, with gender roles varying along ethnic lines.

The various agriculture systems differ in their sustainability and their impact on the aquatic ecosystems of the area. Swidden agriculture and cattle ranching have caused deforestation, and the use of agrochemicals in these systems has resulted in the contamination of the rivers with toxins. The failure to retain a forest buffer along waterways has resulted in sedimentation of the lagoon and the warming of streams. The warming and pollution of rivers could have serious effects on the numerous species of fish and invertebrates that use the rivers to reproduce. Intercropping of fruit and timber trees is both more sustainable than other systems and provides a diversity of products for consumption and retail.

As fishing markets open, less attention is being paid to agriculture. Nietschmann (1972), for example, reports that Miskitu inhabitants turned from farming to turtle fishing with the beginning of a strong market for turtle meat in the early 1970s.

## Forestry

Rates of deforestation and the actual extent of forest in Nicaragua are not consistently reported (Corrales et al. 1996; FAO 1997), but there is a general consensus in published reports that the rate of deforestation is increasing. Nitlapán's (1993) estimates that deforestation along the agriculture frontier is progressing at a rate of about 175 000 ha per year (representing a minimum loss of approximately 2.9% of all of Nicaragua's forest along that front annually) is higher than the figure from the Food and Agriculture Organisation (FAO 1997). It places Nicaragua's deforestation rate near the average for Central America, where Belize has the lowest rate (0.3%) and El Salvador (3.3%) and Costa Rica (3.0%) the highest.

Historically, coast residents relied heavily on rainforest resources for medicines and food. However, the arrival of the Europeans in the 16th century changed the status of the rainforest dramatically — from a source of materials for subsistence needs and a regional trade economy to a source of raw materials for a global economy. The timber of the lowland rainforest became one of the most important commodities for the Europeans and North Americans operating on the coast. This continued through the 19th and 20th centuries as foreign logging companies exploited valuable timber species, such as mahogany (*Swietenia macrophylla*) and crabwood (*Carapa guianensis*) (Parsons 1955; Vernooy 1992, 1995). In many areas, these species have been almost extirpated due to intensive exploitation.

The most common cooking fuel in Nicaragua is wood, but charcoal use is increasing. Wood is taken mainly from areas of secondary growth of mangroves, savanna, and rainforest. The making of charcoal is a common economic activity for Mestizos living in the Rocky Point area. The dense wood of almendro (*Dipteryx panamensis*) is the preferred tree for producing charcoal.

Dories are made of hollowed-out logs taken from the rainforests. Most trees large enough for hulls are now only available in remote reaches of the rivers. The scarcity of suitable trees for boats is a local concern.

Pine forests cover a total area of 500–593 thousand ha in Nicaragua (Corrales et al. 1996). The history of large-scale commercial pine logging on the coast began in the late 1800s and continued into the 1960s, when U.S. companies received concessions (Parsons 1955). In the 1950s, the average annual production exceeded 20 million board feet (Taylor 1962), with a peak of almost 40 million board feet in 1952 (Parson 1955). This level of exploitation, generally without reforestation, led Parsons (1955, p. 57) to remark, "The life expectancy of the coastal pine forests of the Miskitu shore cannot exceed a few years." Most of the best-quality timber was exported to Europe, with the coarser-grained product going to Caribbean markets in Cuba, Jamaica, and Panama. The majority of activity was on the northern coast where the largest tracts of pine savanna are found.

Timber production has been increasing in the last couple of decades, with a slight downturn in the 1980s and a recent notable increase. Clearly, the forests of the coast are entering a period of renewed exploitation. Nicaragua's forestry sector has increasingly come under the scrutiny of environmentalists. They have forced the rejection of a logging concession to Taiwanese interests that was likely to be approved by the Chamorro administration, and placed the issue on the government's agenda.

Logging concessions on state lands are granted by MARENA. According to the Autonomy Statute, the regional councils are to be involved in the concession process on the coast. Commercial cutting on communal lands in Pearl Lagoon also requires the approval of the mayor who charges a tax. However, harvesting by members of the community for fuel wood or materials for houses is not regulated or taxed.

Historically, the taxes, or "purse" as it is called locally, generated from commercial logging on communal lands were used for community development projects such as schools and roads. Most of this money reportedly was used to improve the town of Pearl Lagoon, a cause of tension between communities who felt that the funds should be divided equitably. Typically, local people complain that the concession granting process is controlled by powerful interests and that little of the revenue from today's logging activities remains on the coast.

In general, the accessible forests of Pearl Lagoon are still recuperating from the devastation caused by Hurricanes Joan in 1988 and César in 1996, and from historic large-scale logging operations. Ultimately, however, expanding agriculture is having

44

the strongest influence on Pearl Lagoon's forests. The agricultural frontier has almost reached the southern portion of the lagoon as the settlement of Kukra Hill spreads. Also, newcomers are drawn to the established immigrant communities along the Patch, Wawashang, and Kurinwas rivers. A common cycle, especially in the Wawashang River basin, is for landless peasants to clear small parcels of land in the forest, farm them until soil fertility drops, then sell the parcels to cattlemen from the interior of Nicaragua for use as pasture. Other people are involved in small-scale logging, in which most of the lumber is for local consumption.

A number of activities, such as the collection of medicinal plants and hunting, depend on the presence of forests. Recent studies show that people on the coast still use up to 34 species of plants for medicinal purposes, many of which are rainforest species (Barrett 1994a,b), although knowledge about medicinal plant use is declining as elders pass away (Nickerson 1995). Other species utilized commercially include (Indian) almond seeds, cashew nuts, gourds, pepper, and peach palm fruits. Although hunting is of marginal commercial interest on the coast, it remains an important subsistence activity (Nickerson 1995). In Tasbapauni in the 1970s, 15% of Miskitu men were principally involved in hunting, while an additional 20% hunted and trapped turtles (Nietschmann 1973). In Haulover, few people rely on hunting as a significant source of income. Rather, they treat hunting primarily as a means to supplement their family's diet, with occasional sales of surplus meat.

Nietschmann's (1972, 1973) research is the most detailed account of one Miskitu community, Tasbapauni. The choice of hunting areas and quarry is influenced by dietary preferences, density of animals, seasonality, and market opportunities. In general, the most important hunting grounds are swamps and abandoned or new agricultural fields. Animals are hunted both for their meat and to prevent crop damage: a considerable problem for many farmers who do not live near their fields which are surrounded by forest.

Nickerson (1995) provides one of the few contemporary studies of hunting in Pearl Lagoon. Most hunting is done at night with the use of a flashlight to spot the animal's eyes. Some modern arms left over from the war are used, but most hunting arms are old shotguns and rifles that have been repaired innumerable times and hidden when necessary, such as during the war when personal arms were prohibited.

Recent impressions and interviews with local hunters in Haulover indicate that desirable quarry, such as white-tailed deer (*Odocoileus virginiana*), white-lipped peccary (*Tayassu pecari*), and collared peccary (*Tayassu tajacu*), are returning to pre-Hurricane Joan levels, possibly due to increased amounts of forage as fruiting trees have recovered. Alternatively, it is also possible that as the agriculture frontier reaches Pearl Lagoon, it is driving animals ahead to the remaining forests, thus increasing their densities.

## Toward a better understanding of critical linkages

In this dynamic coastal environment, the terrestrial and aquatic ecosystems are interrelated. Many ecological relationships in the lagoon are largely dependent on the quality of water in the inflowing rivers. Deforestation of river watersheds by agriculture or logging will result in increased sediment loads that could fill in and eliminate productive bottom communities. For example, as benthic organisms that cannot tolerate sedimentation are negatively affected, fish that depend on this food source will also decline. Heavy levels of sedimentation could also physically change the currents and the exchange of fresh and saltwater within the lagoon, which could in turn alter the ecology.

Farmers, hunters, and loggers, whose activities are largely within the terrestrial ecosystems, are indirectly linked to the fishery as it is currently the most active economic sector and is providing capital for the purchase of their products. If the fishery is being overexploited — as many people believe — and collapses, it will have repercussions in the area's forest and agricultural systems as people begin to search for other economic opportunities or return to subsistence farming. Similar connections can be found between other ecosystems of the area. Therefore, it is fundamental to the sustainability of the area that local people, leaders, managers, and scientists carefully examine these critical linkages when making management decisions.

# III

# NO LIFE WITHOUT FISH: A LOCAL HISTORY OF FISH RESOURCES AND THEIR USE

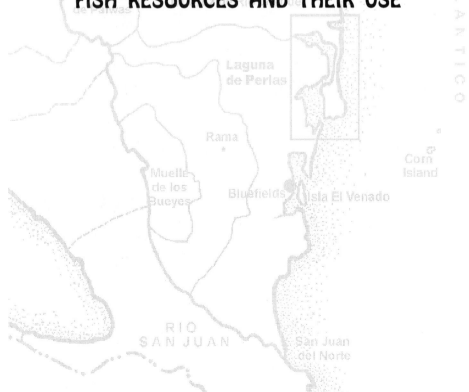

Photo: IDCA

# 3.
# NO LIFE WITHOUT FISH:
# A LOCAL HISTORY OF FISH RESOURCES AND THEIR USE

*Noreen White, Eduardo Tinkam, Mark Hostetler, Ronnie Vernooy*

In chapter 2, we described the Pearl Lagoon basin very much from the perspective of an outsider. This chapter focuses on the people and natural resources of the region from the point of view of its inhabitants. Their account provides additional insights and elicits a number of the themes that are the subjects of the following chapters — the ups and downs in the fisheries sector and related changes in the relation between fishing for domestic and local use and for commercial purposes; changes in technology and their impact; the role of women; resource depletion and environmental issues; and local answers to resource use problems.

We see how the lagoon's fisheries resources and their use have changed over time and continue to change. The history builds on a series of conversations and interviews with key informants from Pearl Lagoon, including George Allen, fisher and communal leader of Haulover; Larry Fox, DIPAL promoter; Ortego Garth, fisher; Melida González, fisher; Carton Moody, fisher; Oswaldo Morales, CAMPlab member, Haulover; Maura Rigby, farmer, Pearl Lagoon; Cloyd Williams, farmer, Pearl Lagoon; and Mauramartha Zeas, former staff member of the NGO, Norwegian Popular Aid. Their insights have been combined into a single story, structured around a number of themes and edited by the authors. Original transcripts were respected as much as possible.

To provide additional views on some of the changes that have taken place in the fisheries sector, we have included a number of newspaper articles throughout the chapter (translated from Spanish by Ronnie Vernooy). These are from the renowned coastal newspaper *La Información*. An important source of local news for decades, this newspaper was published in Bluefields, by and for Costeños (Vernooy 2000). (Other publications on the history of the fisheries sector include Yih (1986), CIDCA (1989), Kasch et al. (1989), Gordon (1991), INDERA (1991), and White (1993).)

The rest of this chapter belongs to the people of Pearl Lagoon.

## Artisanal and commercial exploitation

More than five decades ago, private companies, both national and international, started fishing the Caribbean coast of Nicaragua. Since then, the fleet has increased considerably, although with some ups and downs. For example, in 1988 Hurricane Joan destroyed or damaged many boats and, as a consequence, fish harvests decreased. However, the fisheries sector was reactivated by the central government of Nicaragua, through the Instituto Nacional de la Pesca (INPESCA; the National Fishery Institute). Currently, the sector is controlled by the central government through the Ministry of Economy and Development (MEDE) and the Ministry of Natural Resources and Environment (MARENA). INPESCA no longer plays a role.

### Pesca Nicaragüense company initiates a vital industrial activity in Bluefields — the benefits for Bluefields are positive

A new company, Pesca Nicaragüense (Pescanica), has established an industry that is typical for Bluefields, but one that has never been fully exploited: large-scale fisheries in our rivers and sea, where shellfish and fish are so abundant. These species were underexploited, mainly caught for local consumption in small quantities. For example, shrimp were only caught in their first stage of development due to a lack of initiative by our coastal businessmen.

Shrimp were always caught only for local consumption, in the shallower parts of our bay. However, when fully grown in terms of size and taste, the shrimp would move to deeper waters and the exit to the sea, making it impossible for our fishermen to catch them with their rudimentary boats and fishing gear.

Pescanica is especially equipped for fishing for shark, which are abundant in our sea — it is astonishing how these sharks reproduce. The company has eight modern, powerful, and well-equipped shark-fishing boats, one shrimp-fishing boat, one lobster-fishing boat with a capacity to store 7000 pounds of shrimp, another boat with refrigeration and a laboratory, and the mother-ship Susan, which transports shark oil and other products to the USA and brings back food and other goods that the company uses, including frozen fruits and ice cream, prepared with modern and hygienic methods, and sold in town to the great delight of the local population.

Thanks to the company, a considerable number of workers are able to support their families. Not only do they receive a decent salary, they also are well treated by the manager, Mr William Gaisford, and the other company bosses. The company's monthly payroll is 20 thousand cordobas.

This new company has a magnificent future bringing prosperity to Nicaragua and Bluefields that now can count on a source of income from one of its underexploited resources. [*La Información*, 22 December 1948, p. 12]

### North American businessman, Jack Darling, visits Bluefields showing interest in buying fish and skins of all kinds

For the last few days, North American businessman, Jack Darling, has been in Bluefields, where he is staying at the El Patio guest house. We know from a reliable source that Mr Darling has come to this region to establish a fish exporting business, for which he would buy from local fishermen in large amounts. He has already initiated contacts to obtain sufficient ice to preserve the fish. We also know that Mr Darling will buy lizard, deer, snake, and wari skins for export.

We hope that this industry will become established properly. It would be of great relief and help to local fishermen who always have been obliged to catch only small quantities to satisfy the limited local demand and who do not have the chance to export or trade regionally in this product that is so abundant in our waters. [*La Información*, 6 August 1951, p. 1]

Fishing on the Caribbean coast of Nicaragua focuses on shrimp and scale fish. For communities along rivers, lagoons, and the coast, both artisanal and industrial fishing are economically important. Most of the population's income is derived from fishing. In addition, artisanal fishing provides the communities with a balanced diet, rich in nutrients, protein, and vitamins.

The fishing grounds of the Pearl Lagoon basin consist of a series of lagoons and a continental shelf endowed with small coral keys. The fresh and saltwater ecosystems support a wide variety of aquatic species suitable for exploitation. Traditionally, small-scale fishing has been the main economic activity in Pearl Lagoon. Most is on an artisanal scale, although during the peak season for scale fish and shrimp, fishers catch more than enough for daily consumption and surpluses are sold. At this time, a fisher can easily harvest 90 kg (200 pounds) of scale fish, and approximately 270 kg (600 pounds) of shrimp. Unfortunately, the market is not dependable, especially for fish caught in the lagoon, although the Mar Caribe company buys produce.

Traditional agriculture is also practised in the area. Currently, Mestizo farmers are extending the agricultural frontier. Their migratory methods are causing problems, as deforestation and erosion have a great impact on the aquatic ecosystem of the area.

Furthermore, people of the Pearl Lagoon basin are gradually abandoning their farms and turning to full-time fishing. Farmers argue that the country's economic situation and the lack of a strategy to develop farming systems oblige them to turn to an activity with a quicker payback.

This rapid change from one activity to the other has affected the natural environment of the communities along the basin. As more people turn to fishing, the pressure on the fishing grounds is increasing, and the need for conservation becomes greater.

## Changes

Fish, shrimp, and other aquatic species have been abundant in the Pearl Lagoon area. According to local fisher people, this abundance was due to traditional management practices and people fishing for local consumption. Until recently, there were no processing plants in the basin, and the exchange of agricultural products for fish did not require large-scale fishing. Furthermore, aquatic species were caught using hooks and lines, cast nets, and harpoons. Used rationally, this equipment was not considered destructive to the resources of the lagoon.

Although most shrimp was caught for local consumption, during the early 1960s, small private boats from Bluefields began to come up to the Pearl Lagoon basin to buy white shrimp. They visited all the communities of the basin, but most produce was purchased in the town of Pearl Lagoon and Orinoco.

### Fishing company stops operating in this city — American Fisheries lost more than US $7000

This week Mr Sebastián Agliano left by plane for Managua on his way to Tampa, Florida. Mr Agliano is the director of American Fisheries, the strong fishing company that operated for several months in this city [Bluefields], investing several thousand cordobas in refrigeration and other goods, and employing many local men and women — a flow of money that was of great help to the depressed local economy.

Although the company lost more than US $7000 in Bluefields' shrimp industry, we know that staff of the company are planning to return next September to continue operations because the company's temporary withdrawal is more due to a market collapse abroad. On their return, they will bring heavy-duty refrigerators.

However, we also know that Mr Agliano met with the group of fishermen to settle on a reduced price for the shrimp, but the fishermen did not give in to this request. Despite the negative reply, Mr Agliano spoke well of the fishermen. He said that they are hard-working people and that they always make their point with strength of mind, but are well-mannered and well-educated. [*La Información*, 1 June 1959, p. 1]

### Lobster industry will die if no limit is established on illegal fishing
*by Beltrán Bustamante O.*

The public knows that the lobster industry in Corn Island will come to an end after 4 years of uninterrupted, uncontrolled fishing — of year-long unlimited exploitation.

Never before has Corn Island had the opportunity to exploit its enormous marine wealth located in its keys close to the coast. Thousands of lobsters are caught every day in cages, bringing good profit to the fishermen given that the price per lobster is two cordobas.

But now the relevant question is: why will the lobster fishing come to an end in Corn Island?

Mr Charles Robb, expert on this topic, explained to me that the end of the lobster and shrimp industry is imminent if the relevant ministry does not react quickly and drastically against the barbarian and constant exploitation of these resources by fishermen and buyers. He also explained, as one could expect, that there are months of the year when the fish reproduce and lay eggs, during which it should be prohibited to catch fish. However, he stated, today the catch of lobster and shrimp continues all year without restriction or control, and even illegally as is well known by all coastal people. He added that in catching female lobster before they produce eggs, or taking out the eggs and selling the "cleaned" lobsters to the buyers, the fishermen are contributing to millions and millions of lost animals each year.

Moreover, foreign vessels are entering our sea to catch lobster. A few weeks ago, a pirate boat without refrigeration and with **1000** cages was fishing close to Corn Island. After several days, the boat was forced by our coast guard to abandon Nicaraguan waters, but carrying with it, its containers almost full, the coastal wealth. The most unusual thing of all was that the captain stated that HE DID NOT KNOW that he was fishing in Nicaraguan waters! Imagine, dear readers, what kind of captain this is who does not know in what waters he is lowering his cages... and how ingenuous that we believe him!

We also know from a reliable source that foreign fishermen catch pre-egg-producing female lobsters to sell, not only the meat, but also the eggs, which are in great demand and bring a good price in markets that they know well. And in the face of so much iniquitous exploitation and extermination, nobody is saying "this belongs to us!" Reason? Let's try to find out, Vargas...!

Given this situation, what can we expect? Nothing! We can only confirm that the lobster industry will indeed die soon if no immediate halt is put to so much abuse. The same is true for the shrimp industry in Bluefields. To avoid this coming tragedy, the Ministry of Economy and Natural Resources has the solution in its hands.

There are likely techniques for catching only male lobsters of normal seize and returning young females to the sea so that they can develop and reproduce, and then be caught during periods when the law stipulates. But will the law be respected? Would it be possible that customs officers remain on board of the vessels to monitor legal practice? The above-mentioned ministry has the final word in this sad issue that concerns the Atlantic coast. [*La Información*, 24 September 1963, p. 2]

Later, two businessmen, one French and one Japanese, came to Pearl Lagoon to buy fresh and processed seabob shrimp. In Haulover, a businessman from Managua began doing the same. The price for a can of seabob shrimp was 5 cordobas, which attracted more people to fishing. However, because seabob are in season only twice a year (May–June and September–October) and only for a short time, local people continued to both fish and farm. During the fishing season, when more shrimp were caught than the three businessmen wanted, local people processed their own produce and sold it to other businessmen and women from Managua.

The price of shrimps also affected women's participation in fishery activities, although this was mainly confined to processing and commercialization of the produce.

In the late 1960s, local businessmen began buying white shrimp and selling it to companies in Bluefields (for example, the Booth Company), in the harbour village of El Bluff, and in Schooner Cay (where the Pescanica and Copesnica companies had built warehouses). These local entrepreneurs, who were mainly from Tasbapaunie, Pearl Lagoon, and Marshall Point, owned small inboard motor boats.

### Future operations of the Booth-Nicaragua Fishing Company in the Bluff will include many local workers

Mr A.J. Ruppel, general manager of the new Booth-Nicaragua Company, recently signed a contract with the Bluefields branch office of the National Bank, allowing the company to start operations in the Bluff next month.

As we have been informed, the company will be able to provide its 30 ships with 20 tons of ice daily to store 25 thousands pounds of fish a day and keep more than 150 pounds in stock.

In our next edition, we will write about preparations that the company is planning for the Bluff, including contracting a majority of local fisher people.

Members of the Booth-Nicaragua board of directors are: Mr R.P. Fletcher, President; Mr C.A. Linder, Vice-President; Dr Salvador Castillo, Secretary; Mr A.J. Ruppel, General Manager. The young Carlos Ramírez Aubert will head the accounting department and Mr Urbano Ayala the packing department. [*La Información*, 30 September 1963, p. 4]

### It is said that Mr David Soihet will become the director of Pescanica

To celebrate Easter in this city [Bluefields], the distinguished gentleman David Soihet arrived from Managua. Mr Soihet, a good friend of this newspaper, was a guest of honour of his highly esteemed political friends Dr Manuel Maradiaga Dávila and his wife. Mr Soihet returned to his home in the capital on Thursday, the day before yesterday.

We learned, without being able to confirm it, that Mr Soihet will become the director and manager of the well-known fishing company Pescanica that has been operating for several years now in the region. The company has its head office on Schooner Cay, not far from the mouth of the Escondido River. This news has been received with pleasure and optimism because Mr David is a very energetic person with wide-ranging business experience. He is also well loved on the Atlantic Coast for his altruism, his gentlemanliness and the frank friendship that he shares with all the people that work for him and his personal friends. We greet our beloved friend and we hope that the news that is going around is true. [*La Información*, 1 April 1967, p. 1]

### The impact of fishing practices

Most boats used in the lagoon are made of wood, although some are fiberglass. The 4.5–7 m boats are called canoes and are mainly powered by paddle and sail. A few people have canoes with outboard motors. The size of boat depends on the fishing area, the ability of the owner to catch and store fish, and the duration of fishing.

The gear used for fishing in the lagoon includes hooks and lines, gill nets, shrimp nets, and sometimes harpoons. Until the early 1980s, hook and line fishing was the most common method, and was used in rivers, lagoons, and sometimes in swamps.

Depending on the fishing zone, lines may have different diameters (30–35 mm) and lengths (2–100 m). Hooks also vary with the weight of the target fish. Fishers tend to use fishing line more often during the dry season when waters are clear. According to local knowledge of conservation, fishing lines can be used safely without destroying the ecosystem and the biodiversity of the lagoon.

The early 1970s saw the beginning of great changes in the fisheries resources when a company from Corn Island (Promarblue) came to the basin to fish. A new technique was introduced: gill net fishing. According to the local people, gill netting is a destructive method. Furthermore, gill nets trap fish of all sizes, including those too small to be commercially useful.

Although local fishers did not approve of the use of gill nets, a few received free gear from Promarblue. The large number of fish caught using this method caused more and more fishers to begin using gill nets. People even learned to make the nets by hand, and today, gill nets are the most popular fishing gear used in the Pearl Lagoon basin.

### Three more boats for Promarblue — and a North American fisheries expert is working on Corn Island
*A report by Ruplin*

Taking advantage of a trip that we made to beautiful Corn Island concerning business matters of the Promarblue company and the La Salle printing house (whose motto is "To do the Coastal work on the Coast"), we noticed the strong and promising push that the powerful and modern fishing company Promarblue is giving to the fisheries industry on the Coast, following a small lay-off of employers and an office reorganization.

The management of the company is now in the hands of Mr Alfonso González, who has a degree in Business Management from a prestigious university in the USA. As we were able to observe during our visit to the Promarblue company, Mr González is very talented to run such a complex office. We had trouble carrying on our conversation with the licenciado, as his employers and friends are calling him affectionately, as he was constantly answering phone calls from the island, the rest of the country, and from abroad.

We learned that the company only used to process produce from the Marítima Mundial and Pesca de la Mar companies that were operating in the region with small boats and supplies from Promarblue. Now that the company is in the hands of General Anastasio Somoza Debayle, however, the company has its own fleet and will completely dedicate itself to fishing and processing. Mr Don Dean, a USA fishery expert, was also contracted.

Three new boats, two from Honduras and one from the USA, were delivered by one of the company's high-ranked employers, Mr Oreste Gutiérrez Vado.

The expert Mr Dean told us that he is supervising eight coastal people whom he is teaching and training to become captains and sailors. He added that there is a wealth of fisheries resources in this sea, which he was able to verify himself when on his first fishing trip he caught 17 thousands pounds in 11 days of work, and this with an inexperienced crew and limited gear. We can easily imagine what the catch will be once these young fellows have been trained properly. Mr Dean is very satisfied with the work of his pupils, whom he is also teaching how to use a simple electronic sounding system to locate fishing schools. Mr Dean has two small motor sails named Joseph Faulkner and July and Polly to catch yellow tail. [*La Información*, 23 October 1972, pp. 1,6]

Thus, gill nets are relatively new in the Pearl Lagoon basin. These nets are being used to fish both for local consumption and commercially. The nets vary in length from 45 to 68 m, and are 1.5–3.6 m wide depending on the depth of the fishing area. Gill nets are set in the evening and collected the following morning, about 12 h later. The method is used in all seasons, but most often during the dry season.

Local people argue that there is a clear difference in quality between the fish caught with fishing lines and gill nets. Fish caught in gill nets have drowned by the time the nets are taken out of the water, whereas fish caught with a hook and line are landed fresh. In addition, according to local people, the introduction of gill nets is inefficient in terms of environmental management; they do not allow for much control over the catch.

Shrimp nets are normally used in the shallow waters of the lagoon. The most common nets are 1.5 m in radius and 1.5 m high, with approximately 120 rings. Shrimp nets are made locally by fisher people.

Harpoons are primitive instruments used in areas where other methods are inconvenient for catching large fish. They are also made by local people. Harpoons and fishing lines are the traditional equipment used some 30 years ago in communities of the Pearl Lagoon basin. However, these methods are not practical for commercial fishing.

### Women's roles

In contrast with the rest of the Caribbean coast, in the Pearl Lagoon basin, fishing is not considered strictly a man's activity. Despite inequalities between men and women,

women are active in fisheries. For example, in the Garifuna community of Orinoco, they are as involved in fishing as men. In light of this, a Norwegian NGO, Norwegian Popular Aid, started a women's fishing cooperative to help fisher women. This project provided the cooperative with a meeting place for its members as well as storage facilities for the catch. Women in other communities are also active in the fish trade, selling fish and shrimp locally.

Many women also try to engage in commercial activities outside the community to develop their economic independence and, to some extent, give them political status. Although this is viewed as natural, women continue to face great difficulties in selling their catch outside their own community. On one hand, the traditional subordinate role of women does not allow them to invest much time in economic activity. On the other hand, and even more problematic, religion and the persistence of certain attitudes and opinions regarding family behaviour and relationships contribute to a social consciousness that views women as subordinate.

Thus, tasks are assigned to men and women based on what is supposed to be their domains. Although the fisher women may participate in commerce within the community, they are unlikely to sell their catch to processing companies. Some try to do this, but they are at a disadvantage.

### Not many women employed by the fishing companies in this region — is this because of the winter or is the marine fauna in agony?

It is not without certain alarm that for about 3 weeks now we have been observing, early in the morning, small groups of female employees who work for the fishing companies as cleaners, peelers and packers etc., returning home sad and worried, because the fishing companies are telling them that there is no work for them due to a shortage of produce: the shellfish catch has been zero.

As a result, these workers, who used to earn a modest living, are experiencing bitter moments as they are unable to pay the expenses of their poor and mostly large families with numerous young children.

We hope that the shortage of work for these women is only temporary due to the hard winter period. Because we really do not want to think that the these layoffs are caused by a shrimp fauna already in its last agony, as are the lobster and turtle fauna due to the continuous, voracious and unheard-of exploitation to which they have been subjected for many years, without giving them rest or a chance to reproduce biologically. Prohibition laws have never been implemented, as is the practice all over the world to save the natural wealth of the sea.

But most regrettably, how would we, coastal natives, react if our marine fauna is at the point of dying — as our lumber industry has already done — and never will our communal institutions be able to receive even a single penny of taxes from these costal resources? Likely, as is tradition, we will remain SILENT in the light of such an unjust reality that is confronting us! [*La Información*, 31 August 1974, pp. 1,4]

### Acopiadoras

During the first years of the Sandinista government, a fisheries institute (INPESCA) was created to respond to the lack of markets for fish products. INPESCA regularly sent boats to the Pearl Lagoon area to buy fish. However, in the mid-1980s, when the civil war was at its peak, the boats stopped coming to the area. Later, intermediary buyers, mainly from the Pacific region, came to the communities and traded fish products for a while.

When local people complained they were being underpaid, the Sandinistas organized them into cooperatives to set up small storage facilities (*acopiadoras*). After accumulating a sufficient amount of produce, these acopiadoras sold it to fishing companies in Bluefields. These storage centres did not operate for long, mainly because they were unable to store large enough quantities, and by the time they reached the markets in Bluefields they had spent more on travel than they received for their produce.

In the 1980s, the Sandinista government promoted a new policy to benefit fisher people. Fishers were organized into various kinds of cooperatives. Through state-owned fishing companies, the cooperatives received fishing gear and ice to preserve the catch. Periodically, fishing boats from companies in Bluefields arrived to buy the produce of the basin. According to fishers, this practice was not considered destructive of the resource base, as only local people were involved in fishing and they kept control of the situation.

During the early 1990s, Pearl Lagoon basin became one of the most popular areas for exploitation by private fisheries enterprises, which were also known as acopiadoras. Four storage facilities were built and equipped for buying and processing produce from both the lagoon and the sea. Among these enterprises were a company owned by a local Creole man from Pearl Lagoon and the Fishermen Union Stock Centre, owned by the fishing cooperative of Haulover and Pearl Lagoon.

Currently, only two acopiadoras are based in the basin. One of them is Mar Caribe, the biggest and most successful company, which is owned by a Creole man from Corn Island. The other is the Fishermen Union Stock Centre, which is functioning with some financial and organizational constraints. In addition, a boat (the *Sunrise*) sometimes comes from Bluefields to buy fish. The establishment of Mar Caribe was considered the answer to the lack of a market for fish products.

The acopiadoras provide the fishermen (women do not sell to them) with ice, fuel, and some fishing gear and, in return, the fishermen sell their produce to the acopiadora. For some time, Mar Caribe also served as a link between DIPAL and the fishermen. DIPAL leased fishing gear and other equipment to fishermen, then billed Mar Caribe, which deducted the cost of the gear from the money paid for the fish. However, DIPAL has ceased this practice.

When the two acopiadoras are working at full capacity, fishers have the opportunity to sell their produce every day. This is increasing pressure on the lagoon, which is a growing concern. In addition, fishers from other areas (i.e., Bluefields, Corn Island, and Kukra Hill) are fishing more frequently in the Pearl Lagoon basin, and some Mestizos, who are not traditionally fishers, are also fishing in the basin.

## Growing concerns

The incursion of fisher people from other parts of the region, and now Mestizos, into the basin is alarming local people. The situation is considered a threat to both the people of the basin and to the resources. On one hand, local people argue that the fisher population of the Pearl Lagoon basin is already high. Many farmers are now fishing, because of the immediate income the activity brings, and the younger generation is following their example. In some communities, boys are dropping out of school to earn money by fishing and increase their family's income.

On the other hand, a group of people in the basin consider that all Nicaraguans have the right to fish in the lagoon, although they agree that the catch and the number of nets should be controlled. In addition, those who think fishers should be free to fish in the lagoon recognize that even local populations can have a negative impact on the ecosystems in which they live through overuse and poor management of their natural resources. This argument is based on current changes in local people's lifestyles and their unsustainable exploitation of resources.

The recent phase of exploitation of fisheries resources for commercial purposes has had a significant impact on the communities of the Pearl Lagoon basin. Local people who depended on both agriculture and fishing are now focusing only on fishing. And where fishing was carried out at a subsistence level, now it is considered a solution to the people's economic problems.

To residents of the lagoon, having to wait 3–4 months, and in some cases even a year, to harvest crops seems a long time compared with the immediate rewards of fishing. Thus, sooner or later farmers abandon their fields to take up fishing. As a result, people of the basin are becoming more and more dependent on such products as rice, roots, and tubers from other parts of the country.

### A serious problem: the exaggerated exploitation of shrimps
*by Andrew Hebbert Downs*

Thanks to reports received from the fishermen who catch turtles in the Caribbean, we know about the customs, lifestyles, and movements of one of the most persecuted marine species on the Atlantic Coast of Nicaragua.

It is well known that until January the turtles feed in the Pearl Lagoon keys and then they move northeast toward the keys known as Tyre and Man O War. From March to May, you will find them feeding in the strong waves in front of the Grande River and Sandy Bay shorelines. However, during the reproduction period from June to August, they will move to the south toward Costa Rican waters. It may seem strange, but although the turtles pass the year in Nicaraguan waters, they do not breed or lay eggs on the Atlantic Coast.

Taking these facts about the turtles into account, some questions arise: What do we know about the habits, reproduction and movements of the shrimp that live in our waters? When do they lay eggs? Where do they do this? If we do not know anything about these shrimp, we will never be able to protect effectively this industry that is so important to our economy no matter how many laws the legislative chambers pass.

For example, let us assume that a law to protect the turtles during their reproduction period is declared. It would be useless because during this time the turtles are not in Nicaraguan waters, but in Costa Rican waters. We know that our waters are not appropriate for the reproduction of this species due to climatic conditions. How would it be for the shrimps?

It would be convenient if the honourable Minister of the Environment were to open an office in Bluefields to study the movements, reproduction areas, etc., of the shrimp before the government passes a law to protect this shellfish from the continuous exploitation that could put an end to this national resource. This study would take about 2 years.

The large number of rivers that flow into the ocean on the Atlantic Coast carry with them an enormous amount of cold water coming from the continuous rains that fall in our department, and this leads to a more or less constant cold water temperature that is not appropriate for the reproduction of turtles. That is why they move south. What is happening, we repeat, with the shrimp? [*La Información*, 22 February 1969, pp. 1,6]

## Local knowledge about the protection of fisheries resources

Most people from the Pearl Lagoon basin are conscious of the need to protect their fisheries resources. People feel that the fish are not as abundant as they were in the past (when people fished at a subsistence level or for trade within the communities of the basin). In addition, awareness has increased since people have been receiving training regarding their environment and how to take care of and use their natural resources in more sustainable ways. In this sense, local people have also increased the demand for environmental protection.

Currently, there is a strong belief among the people of the Pearl Lagoon basin that to protect the resources of the lagoon and the sea, they must implement a management plan. The local people also know that protecting fish resources means protecting the forest as well. According to them, there is a close relation between the lagoon and the forest; if the forest is destroyed, the fish and shrimp will also perish. In addition, local people consider that strategies, such as returning to small-scale agriculture and using traditional fishing gear, would decrease the pressure on fish resources. They argue that the communities survived when they used traditional fishing methods and traditional agriculture; thus, it is a matter of readopting their old lifestyle.

In this new phase of awareness, the CAMPlab team has played an important role in training local people in monitoring the forest, fish, and water. The CAMPlab committees of residents in each community also train other local people, mainly in natural resource protection. As a result, local perception of the importance of resource management and environmental protection has increased in the last 5 years.

Although the majority of the population of the Pearl Lagoon basin knows about resource management, some communal leaders do not see the need for resource protection. Although they realize that natural resources are not as abundant as before, they don't believe that the resources of the basin are in danger of overexploitation. Further, they agree that efficient management of revenue from fishing activities could lead to development of the basin.

There is a general agreement that the fish resources are not overexploited, but the constant pressure on the lagoon and the sea could have a negative effect on them. Currently, species, such as snook and coppermouth, are showing signs of depletion.

## The need for a management plan

Local people believe that the implementation of a natural resources management plan is the beginning of the sustainable use of resources. The management plan should limit the number of fishers (especially those who have come recently to fish in the basin); establish the size of mesh of the gill nets (not less than 10 cm); determine where nets should not be set (i.e., the canal); and prohibit trawling, which has had serious negative effects on aquatic species of all sizes.

Diversification is another way to protect fish resources from overexploitation, although this involves seeking markets for nontraditional resources. Even then, the nontraditional species should be exploited in a sustainable manner to prevent depletion.

Local people's awareness of the current situation is the first important step leading to a solution to the environmental problems that affect all communities of the basin. With the knowledge they have acquired over the last 10 years and with the help of projects such as CAMPlab and those of other organizations that have worked in the area, local people believe they can rescue the resources that were once abundant. Furthermore, people are clearly accepting a collective responsibility for the management of their resources and the preservation of their value.

# IV

## "GOING FAR TO CATCH A FISH": LOCAL PERCEPTIONS OF THE DYNAMICS AND IMPACTS OF A CHANGING RESOURCE BASE

Photo: Mark Jamieson

# 4.   "GOING FAR TO CATCH A FISH": LOCAL PERCEPTIONS OF THE DYNAMICS AND IMPACTS OF A CHANGING RESOURCE BASE

*Mark Hostetler*

In this chapter, we build on the local history presented in chapter 3 by focusing on people's perceptions of the impact of the changes in the fisheries in three Pearl Lagoon villages (Haulover, Kakabila, and Orinoco) and their reactions to the changes. This is an example of a largely indigenous rural population trying to deal with the effects of the increasing commercialization of their natural resources, a situation that is common in the lagoon and on the Atlantic coast. It gives us an opportunity to examine the extent to which these communities have the ability and desire to modify the changes — based on local norms and values — in ways that are more equitable and sustainable in socioeconomic and environmental terms. The material in this chapter is based on Hostetler (1998).

## A shift toward the market

Much of the previous work done on the Caribbean coast of Nicaragua on the relations between culture, environment, and the economy stresses the dual forms of the economy that have existed, especially among the Miskitu peoples, for hundreds of years (Helms 1969; Nietschmann 1973). In this socioeconomic organization, which Helms (1969) calls a purchase economy, people have traditionally engaged in both wage- and subsistence-based activities. This arrangement has served the population relatively well as it cushioned "boom" and "bust" cycles, providing at least basic needs during bad times and access to foreign goods in more prosperous times.

Although various resources were exploited during much of this time, the people were not overly concerned about the predominantly extractive industries in the area. MacDonald (1988, p. 122) explains:

The Miskitu's moral economy included both subsistence rights and deep emotional concerns regarding land and resource rights. The cycles of several boom-and-bust economies on Nicaragua's Atlantic coast, while exploitative in other people's minds, generally did not violate that moral economy and so did not cause resentment or violence.

However, the communities became concerned and problems began to occur when this moral economy was threatened. A major way in which this has happened in recent years is through the transfer of subsistence items into the realm of market exchange (Nietschmann 1973). Dozier (1985, p. 230) explains how increased dependence on subsistence items has led to difficulty through

> Overemphasis, in both exploitation and efforts, upon a narrower range of subsistence activities to provide products with the greatest market demand. This could lead not only to depletion of various subsistence resources, but, if in the animal category, to neglect of agriculture. The consequent decline in traditional food production and village sharing could then create more dependence upon bought foods.

The trend toward turning a formerly subsistence good into a commercial product is most noticeable in the turtle fishery along the Atlantic coast. Turtle meat — a major source of dietary protein that was distributed according to social conventions — became an export product that was sold for profit. The result was severe depletion of this resource (Nietschmann 1973; Cattle 1976; Dozier 1985).

The Pearl Lagoon fisheries provide another example of this shift. The increased sale of fish is consistent with the traditional economic patterns of the population in the sense that it provides a socially and culturally necessary source of money. However, it is also creating social problems by upsetting the subsistence economy. The traditional tactic of reverting to a subsistence economy to cushion the effects of a downturn in the cash economy is being gradually undermined by the overexploitation of these fisheries *and* the declining viability of agriculture. While some in the communities may profit from new commercial relations in the fisheries, others suffer as access to these traditional sources of food becomes more difficult.

The lagoon fishery is a central component of the livelihoods of most people of the region. As a result, the continued use of this resource as the major part of the cash economy is unlikely to end. As we saw in chapter 3, however, many people recognize the dangers inherent in overexploitation, and want to control and moderate the fishery to ensure its survival and protect their subsistence security. If the threat to the moral economy becomes more widely recognized, it may prove to be an effective catalyst for significant environmental protection initiatives in the region. However, any efforts to achieve sustainable management of the resources must be based on an understanding of the various factors that influence and motivate their use. In addition, no socially or environmentally sustainable solution is possible without the consent of the majority of the local people.

## Documenting local perceptions

The material in this chapter comes from two sets of interviews conducted in the Pearl Lagoon basin in 1997. In the technique used, both the interviewer and the respondent are viewed as active participants in the construction of knowledge about the experiences of the respondent (Holstein and Gubrium 1995). An interview guide was used, but leeway was given to the respondents to develop topics in ways that were relevant for them. The interviewer did not dictate interpretations to respondents, but did play an active role in bringing alternative considerations to bear, pointing out possible linkages among various experiences of the respondents and suggesting different views of experiences.

The interviews (conducted in Creole English) provide many insights into people's opinions about the issues discussed. Their structure also allowed avenues for exploring the various topics. As a result, they give us a fuller understanding of the complexity of the issues. However, because the interviews deal with people's opinions, they do not necessarily reflect their actions and are not generalizable to the rest of the population.

The first set of interviews was based on a revised version of an interview guide concerning traditional fishing knowledge initiated by Eduardo Tinkam in the community of Haulover (see Annex 1). Interviewees were selected with the help of CAMPlab communal investigators Eduardo Tinkam, Haulover; Ray Garth, Kakabila; and Bonifacio González, Orinoco, on the basis of their experience as fishers. The interviews focused both on the participants' knowledge of the lagoon and lagoon species as well as their opinions about measures that should be taken to protect the lagoon's resources.

The second set of interviews focused on five topics: lagoon production for subsistence rather than for market; the importance of these resources to different groups in the community; the effects of changes in fishing on various community members; potential ways of solving the communities' problems related to fishing; and the different roles of men and women in the communities (see guide in Annex 2). These interviews were also conducted in Haulover, Kakabila, and Orinoco. Four of the participants in the first set of interviews also participated in the second set.

The first participants in the second set of interviews were the CAMPlab communal investigators for each of the three communities. They had a relatively well-rounded view of the situation and a generally high level of education about natural resources because of their participation in workshops and other CAMPlab work. In addition,

**69**

these investigators are known and respected community members (they were all chosen by their communities for their jobs) and they were able to point out people with differing viewpoints and secure interview opportunities. Subsequently, the communal investigators were asked to select further participants with diverse opinions representative of the various viewpoints in their communities; these people were then interviewed.

Although neither random nor reflective of the full range of opinions in the communities, the interviews did capture a relatively broad spectrum of the population. This was somewhat hindered by factors such as time and participant willingness and availability; for example, it was especially difficult to include women in the research. A total of 33 interviews were conducted across social categories of age, class, ethnicity, and gender. The participants included 29 people (8 women and 21 men) ranging in age from 20 to 85 years. Of the 25 participants for whom ethnicity was recorded, 6 identified themselves as Miskitu, 4 as Creole, 4 as a Creole Miskitu mix, and 11 as Garifuna (see also Annexes 3 and 4).

In selecting the responses to include in this chapter, particular attention was paid to the diversity of opinions on each subject. Although everyone's comments cannot be included, all major ideas are presented. Responses are in Creole English with appropriate explanations.

## Changes in the Pearl Lagoon fishery

The major change occurring in the fisheries of Pearl Lagoon is the increasing shift from traditional channels of social distribution and local consumption into the realm of market exchange. This has led to less-equal distribution of these resources and has also intensified exploitation resulting in a series of effects (both positive and negative) on individuals and the communities as a whole.

The major impacts identified by participants in the research can be divided into four categories: a greater focus on fishing at the expense of other economic activities, most notably farming; a decrease in lagoon fish stocks; changes in distribution patterns of fish among the population; and increasing social differentiation. These are discussed below.

## Abandoning agriculture

The reasons for the move from other productive activities, especially agriculture, to fishing are diverse and they differ among the communities studied. The effects include decreased food production for use in the community and increased exploitation of the fisheries resource. More important, this change plays a role in undermining the local subsistence economy by decreasing the ability of these communities to re-engage in subsistence agriculture in the event of an economic downturn.

A variety of explanations for the move away from agriculture were offered by the people interviewed. Probably the most important and most frequently cited relates to access to markets for agricultural produce, i.e., distance to the market, lack of efficient transportation, and unpredictability of demand for the produce. Victor, a 35-year-old fisher from Haulover, illustrated this:

> Victor: First I used to work plantation work but real come out hard for me. When you working plantation work sometime you plant a lot of corns lot of beans and no business for it. Maybe you just have to feed the fowls them and maybe if you raising a pig you feed them also. Then you just have the corn until they take weevils.
>
> Interviewer: So you have no market for it?
>
> Victor: No market and... I prefer fishing because I see in the fishing I make better life for my family.

Winston, a Kakabila man in his early 20s, and Richard, a Orinoco man of the same age, expressed similar ideas:

> Winston: We don't have market so that is why people don't plant the amount that they should plant. Because sometime you have your product and like maybe banana and plantain... and we carry them to Pearl Lagoon and sometime we bring them back over because no market.
>
> Richard: In time gone people used to dedicate a lot to farming. But it come to happen that people see too much of a small result of farming in the community, so people find out that in the fishing it generate more money so people find more importance to go fishing.

These statements reflect the situation of many people in Haulover, Orinoco, and Kakabila. However, the prevailing instability in the markets for farm produce compared with fish has pushed many to rely on the fisheries, where there is now a consistent place to sell. Perhaps the most important issue was many people's contention that fishing, in comparison with agriculture, offers quick access to money. This was made clear by Samuel:

> Interviewer: Somebody else told me that people find fishing easier money.
>
> Samuel: Quick...

Interviewer: Yes, not easier but quick. Do you think that has a big effect?

Samuel: Sure. When I have a problem, like say, I need a book or pencil or shoe, then I don't go to the farm because it take me 9 months.

Albert, an Orinoco fisher in his late 20s, identified the same dynamic, "The most basic thing to buy something or to do something is to fishing or the shrimps." Samuel and Albert reflect the thinking of many people who rely increasingly on fishing. In agriculture, profit is not seen for months, whereas fishing offers the opportunity for people to put money in their pockets tomorrow. Fishing allows people to meet their short-term cash needs effectively.

### Changing women's roles

Another important aspect of the move away from agriculture has been a decline in women's involvement in farm work. Helms (1969) and Weiss (1980) indicated that, traditionally, in Miskitu communities women played a major role in agricultural production. Davidson (1976) reported the same pattern for the Garifuna. While men were more involved in various cash economies, women often tended the family plots — thus maintaining the subsistence part of the household economy. Weiss (1980) showed that women's roles seldom included the initial clearing of land, but that women tended to work in most other phases of production. A study of a Garifuna community in Punta Gorda, Belize, indicates a similar pattern (Cominsky 1976).

This pattern was confirmed in interviews, most of which revealed that women's involvement has declined for a variety of reasons related to children's educational needs, changing attitudes about women's roles, and women's personal preferences. Both interviews and published reports show that this change is more prevalent in Haulover and Orinoco than in Kakabila (Barbee 1997).

Women in Haulover have tended to move away from agriculture to ensure that their children are educated. Lesbia, a 27-year-old Haulover woman, explained:

Lesbia: If him [her husband] going to farm I not going to go be in the bush because my children have to go to school, and if I go back there to sit down maybe I going to raise fowl, and I going to raise hog, and him going farm but then my children not going to get education, and after it end up them is big men and can't write them name. So I have to stay here and give them education.

This situation was also described by a 28-year-old woman from Haulover who added that providing support for men who are participating in fishing is also a factor.

Because plenty men came out to fishing and the children have to go to school and thing like that. So well the women left the farm now and tried to put the children into school, had to cook for the husband so they could go out thing like that.

This factor is important in Haulover, where the largest portion of agricultural land is located 1.5 h away (on foot) in Rocky Point. The women's need to stay in the village of Haulover has also tended to draw men away from the farm, as the same interviewee indicated: "Usually the men if the wife is not with them on the farm they usually come out and they won't stay there anymore."

Children's education was also mentioned as a major reason for women to stop farming and fishing work in Orinoco. Albert, an Orinoco fisher in his late 20s, noted:

Women decide to get more serious and see things more brighter that without education you cannot walk with the right way. So them spend more time at home to tend to them children to send them to class and then the man start to work. So the thing look more prettier then.

Overall, the educational needs of children are probably less a factor for women's move from agriculture in Orinoco than in Haulover, because the agricultural land in Orinoco is much closer to the community. However, this reason was given, possibly because it is linked to the changing views of the role of women in the community.

In Kakabila, children's education was not identified as a factor by any of the respondents. This community is somewhat different, in that agricultural plots are much closer to the community, allowing people to work their lands and live at home without the burden of a 3-h walk each day (Jamieson 1995).

Further contributing to women's move away from agricultural work appears to be a shift in attitudes about women's roles. This was illustrated by a community leader from Haulover, who was quoted by Barbee (1997): "We men these days don't like to see women get into farm and work. Chopping is hard work it is for men not women.... We have great sympathy toward women.... We keep them from the hard work." Similar sentiments were expressed by Winston Brown a Kakabila fisher in his early 20s.

Interviewer: Do you think women work the farm as much as they did in the past?

Winston: No, first women used to work more but not now.

Interviewer: No, why you think that change is?

Winston: Because maybe I believe people are getting wiser you know. First many women they think like men, and now then maybe things are changing. Maybe I take my women and I say I take you and I responsible for you mustn't do hard work and I must do the hard work and things like that.

Although these attitudes are not universal, there is a growing belief in these communities that agricultural work is too hard for women and they should be protected from it. This view tends to be stronger among men than women; however, it is also likely that many women would rather not do farm work.

Women are also tending to look toward education as a way to improve their situation at a younger and younger age. As a result they are shunning agricultural work. Richard, a fisher from Orinoco in his early 20s, pointed out that "women don't want to go to bush, they don't see good result in it." He suggested that if you "take a girl and maybe tell her let us dedicate to farming and maybe she look at you as a crazy person." In the case of Haulover, alternative employment opportunities are available for some at the fish processing plant where approximately 30 Haulover women work for roughly USD 6/day (Christie 1999). Although men in these communities increasingly believe women should not work in agriculture, it also appears that many women do not have much interest in pursuing this activity, if other alternatives are available.

The trend for women to no longer be involved in agriculture has had a variety of effects on the community. It has contributed directly to the erosion of subsistence agriculture because women have traditionally played a major role in the care and maintenance of crops, especially when men are engaged in the cash economy. It has also had an effect on men's agricultural involvement, as men prefer to stay with their families in the village rather than working alone on the farm. On the other hand, abandoning farming has been necessary to facilitate children's education, and opportunities for a few women to earn wages have increased their household incomes.

### Changing attitudes of youth

Attitudes toward the hard work required in farming are changing. Some of the older respondents, like 85-year-old Haulover community leader McKinley, suggested that young people are not inclined to undertake the hard labour involved in farming.

Well there is one reason that the people don't farm, because as I told you, farming not very easy. You have to be a man that aggressive and resolute of mind.... We farm here but brutally because we has no machine, we has nobody to back us up, only machete and ax and hoe... and so on; its not easy. I went through it so I can tell you that.

Charles, a resident of Orinoco in his mid-50s, made similar comments about the situation there:

> Not everybody plant; most of them people, especially the young generation catch a little shrimps. Make a little money to drink their beer and smoke them cigarettes. Everybody trying to give up the forests. Maybe its only me and a couple of mans pick out thems that are real man, [we] try to go out work bush. Nobody want fly to bite them no more. They say its modern, but to me that's not modern.

> Interviewer: Why do you feel that young boys don't want to go out in the bush?

> Charles: Them afraid of bush. Them just lazy, and them say everything is modern now. Man mustn't go in the bush go work. But if he doesn't work in the bush what he going to do? There isn't no company here that you can go by the company to work and support yourself. So you got to support yourself in one way either in the bush or to sea.

Salomen, another Orinoco resident, explained this in a slightly different way, pointing to the effects of increased knowledge of the outside world through contact with people in Bluefields and Pearl Lagoon.

> They look on how the people living there and they what you would call it? They adopt their life them. They adopt the people them life, and Bluefields people no have plantation and they live to the market, and them say them going to work like the people in Bluefields and Pearl Lagoon.

In these communities, where an ax, machete, and hoe are generally the only tools used, farming does not present an attractive option for young people. It is not surprising, then, that young people prefer the idea of modern "city life" relying more on the cash economy. The only work alternative in these communities that resembles this lifestyle is fishing.

A further cause for the move away from agriculture that was mentioned by participants is the decline of collective work, traditionally used to accomplish heavy farm tasks. This practice has been undermined to some extent by the availability of wage labour making it more difficult for some people to engage in farming. Eduardo, a Haulover resident, explained:

> There was a custom around here where women and children would take part in farming. Like they would plant a common ground and even in the community neighbors and other friends would go and help that farmer plant today and tomorrow we would help another farmer.

Interviewer: Why did that change?

Eduardo: That change because money is the case. People start hiring men, hire hands to work on the farm and then that start... if you have more money then myself and you do that type of thing, then I would stay alone to do my work.

The introduction of paid labour for farming appears to be less a factor in Kakabila, where interview participants still talked about communal agricultural efforts like those Eduardo described.

### *Impact of the war*

Also contributing to the decline in agricultural activity in these communities is the residual effects of the Contra war that raged in the mid and late 1980s. Barbee (1997) points to the reluctance of Haulover women to work in agricultural areas, based on wartime events and the fear of robbery or rape. In a similar vein, Bonifacio of Orinoco explained how the war affected agriculture in Orinoco and led to the prolonged inability of people to farm in that community:

> We go to get two sack of dasheen [a tuber crop]. It was like we send out two squad man. And so it's not one man going because you could meet an enemy right there. So people were just scared. So... we would chase a day when we say, who want breadkind will get ready. We send out a troop for the people who want to go to the farm to get breadkind, and you know everybody would just go to that one farm and come home.

The war meant life on the agricultural land of Haulover and Orinoco was dangerous, and lingering fears combined with a lack of continuity in agriculture have played a role in some young people's decisions not to enter this field. These fears were not shared in Kakabila, partly because its agricultural areas are not easily accessible to outsiders, making it less likely for strangers to go there (Barbee 1997).

### *"Farming going waste:" a synthesis*

According to participants, the overall effects of the shift away from agriculture revolve around a number of themes, many of which were articulated by Eduardo Tinkam.

Interviewer: Why does that [less people farming] make you nervous?

Eduardo: Because we could have an overexploitation by farmers becoming fishermen and then too much weight on the fishing. Then we are leaving the farm to go waste. The Spaniards [Mestizos] coming in and taking away the land from the people who leave them lay.

Interviewer: Does it also cut down the amount of food because people don't have their own patch of cassava or plantain?

Eduardo: It causes a drop on the economy because these people are catching fish to simply pay their bills at the stores. When they have the farm they have the farm planted with beans rice corn and these type of things, they don't pay for that, and then they have the fishing food, the fishing product that they can eat. So they would maybe buy clothes when they are doing the two thing at the same time.

Eduardo's concerns were also expressed by people from the other communities. First, most people indicated that the move of many people from farming into fishing has increased the pressure on lagoon resources. Second, for the households that are no longer involved in farming even for personal consumption, the home economy has been diminished. Often much of the profit from fishing is needed to buy products that had previously been grown by the family or relatives to them. Finally, some people feared that abandoning farming was contributing to the encroachment of Mestizos onto community lands, potentially preventing the local people from returning to farming in the future.

As we saw in chapter 3, the move away from agriculture in these communities is caused by a broad range of factors. Most notable is the ease with which they can earn money by selling fish combined with the difficulties involved in selling agricultural products. The shift in production away from agriculture is usual in times of economic boom; however, the current shift from agriculture appears to be less reversible than in the past. This is due to factors such as the encroachment of the agricultural frontier; communal lands left fallow; people's increasing preference for alternatives to agricultural work, especially young people and women; and a decrease in the availability of voluntary collective labour to undertake more difficult tasks.

The shift is contributing to overfishing, and in the current situation, people are less able to return to agriculture, if the fisheries economy is not sustained. The more complete move from the farm means that people are becoming less able to farm in traditional ways (Helms 1971), and the encroachment of Mestizos into the region means that farmlands may not be available in the future (Nietschmann 1973; Cattle 1976).

The abandonment of farming is more serious in Haulover and Orinoco than in Kakabila. Easier access to agricultural lands in Kakabila means that most families maintain significant "plantations" to serve household needs. Although many families in Haulover have plantations, they tend to produce less for household needs than in the past, increasing the community's reliance on the cash economy.

## Decreases in fish stocks

A decline in fish stocks is accompanying the increase in commercialization. When asked about the availability of fish in the lagoon, most people indicated that access to fish was becoming increasingly difficult, and that greater effort was required to catch fish than in the past. Melida and Albert from Orinoco described this:

> Interviewer: You said before it is not so easy to catch coppermouth now?
>
> Melida: Oh no, only with luck you catch about three or four. Once when I used to go up to the place named Holo Myra, I alone [would catch] 35 and 40.
>
> Albert: Today it's something different. It's more scarcer than before. First time all these hours all these fishermen done come in already. Done catch a fish to eat and they don't have to go far. But now I tell you brother you have to go really far to catch a fish to eat.

Interview participants in Kakabila, Haulover, and Orinoco suggested that fish that were once abundant are now difficult to catch. According to many people, fishers have to travel farther and use more equipment. Herman Humpfries of Kakabila explained:

> Interviewer: Are people still using hand lines?
>
> Herman: That doesn't give effect you hardly catch anything on hand line now. The only fish you does catch on hand line around this area is jack and catfish.... You catch one coppermouth, you catch drummer and these sort of fish, but in here it is seldom that you catch one of these fishes if it is not in gill net.
>
> Interviewer: Do people still strike fish?
>
> Herman: People don't strike. You can't see a fish to strike. The fish get so scarce that they doesn't do like first. First the fish would come a time in September we go to the bar there right in front of Mar Caribe, or the other side we call Ker Wake point and... you through your staff whole day if you want... Sometime you strike all 10–15 or something with harpoon and these times you no see one.

Herman expressed a widely held belief that these traditional methods of harvesting lagoon resources are becoming less effective. This change has had the greatest effect on women, who are perceived to be unable to use modern techniques, as well as on less affluent people, who do not possess modern equipment like gill nets and motors.

### Negative impacts on women

In all communities, women who had fished with hand lines to supplement their families' diets have been especially affected by the apparent decline in fish stocks. In Orinoco, women who traditionally fished commercially and have a fishing cooperative, are less able to work. This woman's statement is representative:

> Women hardly does fishing now, because being... to using different gears like gill net, and you have to go farther, and now the first time we just used to use with hand line, and you could go and catch your fish and when the breeze start to come in you come back sailing home and now women hardly go fishing.

In these communities, women are not believed to be capable of handling gill nets or traveling great distances on the lagoon alone, so they are increasingly unable to fish as stocks decline. Gordon (1991) suggests that part of this may be due to the fact that men don't want women to be in competition with them; as a result, they are discouraging women from using gill nets. There is no outright prohibition against women using gill nets, but this type of fishing is widely believed by both men and women to be men's work.

One of the major impacts of these changes is an overall decline in the household economy. An Orinoco women explains:

> You find the situation a little harder now.... The man and woman used to go and catch and they could help. The two of them could help in the daily situation of the home. Meanwhile, sometime the man go on and doesn't catch nothing and either one or the next one do nothing.

Women's decreasing ability to engage in this productive activity decreases family income. In addition, it has an effect on the likelihood of fish being caught by a family member for household consumption, because the women in the family are less likely to be fishing.

One exception to women's declining involvement is in the white shrimp harvest in Orinoco. Albert explains:

> Women go catch shrimps too when it is shrimps time when the shrimps is close round and them get in that dory stand and things go more softly for their family because their partner don't have to share with another person.

In this community, the annual harvest of white shrimp is the most important source of income and, as a result, the whole community becomes heavily involved.

### Role of the gill net

Fishers who do not have the necessary gear (i.e., gill nets and, to a lesser extent, motors) to catch fish commercially are also at a disadvantage. Winston Brown of Kakabila suggested that "maybe if you don't have any gill net, I don't make any money. So that is something important to have because you make money off that." In the past, people were able to catch substantial amounts of fish using a simple hook and line or a harpoon; this is no longer true.

Many attribute the decline in fish stocks to the intensified use of gill nets in the lagoon. It is difficult to establish when exactly the gill net was first introduced into the region, especially as it appears to have occurred at different times in the three communities. However, most people interviewed agreed that intense use by a large segment of the population began only recently. The presence of the Mar Caribe company has contributed to this, both by providing a consistent market for the fish caught and also by providing gill nets. Distribution of fine-mesh nets (6 cm) to fishers by the company has been heavily criticized by community residents, who believe these nets are wasteful and damage future fish stocks by catching juvenile fish.

People from outside Pearl Lagoon, most notably from Bluefields, are also regarded by many in the lagoon as contributing to declining fish stocks. Eduardo from Haulover explained:

> You know Mark, I think people feel a little uneasy about people from Bluefields coming to fish. The people from Bluefields they use new methods of fishing like sinking their nets in the bar [the mouth of the lagoon], and then they use a big amount of nets.... So the people are nervous about the situation, because they feel like this type of fishing, that amount of nets, they could put a heavy pressure upon the resources.... So people are complaining about this.

These outsiders tend to use more nets and more efficient techniques than lagoon people, and this causes concern and resentment among the local residents.

People interviewed also expressed the belief that fishing at certain times (e.g., when fish were about to spawn,) and in certain places (e.g., major spawning locations or migratory roots) was also contributing to the decline in stock. The efficiency of the gill net in catching fish migrating through narrow passages was believed by some to have a major impact on the number of fish in the lagoon.

### Stock decline: a synthesis

The decline in fish stocks is viewed by many in the communities as the result of new types of commercial exploitation in the lagoon. The decline has had two important effects: more effort and better gear are needed to catch comparable amounts of fish; and certain segments of the population are increasingly unable to fish for household consumption or sale.

Fishers must spend more time, travel longer distances, and use more sophisticated gear to catch adequate numbers of fish. This change has increasingly meant that traditional and universally accessible means of exploiting lagoon resources are becoming unreliable.

With their modern gear and with increased efforts by fishers, the commercial parts of the fisheries are flourishing. However, the people are less able to catch fish to supplement their diets, as this usually involves more traditional methods. Overall, the apparent decrease in fish stocks in the lagoon has been a cause for concern for many, but especially those without access to modern equipment. In addition, it is perceived to have had a particular impact on the ability of women to contribute to the household economy through fishing, something that was especially important in Orinoco where women have traditionally been involved in fishing. Some people in the communities have prospered from the use of modern fishing techniques, thereby actively contributing to the decline of fish stocks and making it more difficult for others to obtain these resources.

## "Now everything is money": changes in distribution patterns

Intensive commercialization of the fisheries has led to significant changes in fish distribution patterns. The situation was explained by Eduardo from Haulover and Ray from Kakabila:

> Eduardo: In the past because of a lack of market people would give away most of the fish they capture. Actually [now] the case is different, fishermen would only bring in for themselves and the amount that they bring in is so limited that they can't share this with other people. Its too limited; maybe just good friend they would bring a little fish for. But most of it is sold to the company.

> Ray: First when people use to fishing in this community the fish never use to be sold in the community. It was given away or you make exchange; you give me a fish for some kind of ground food and things like that. Now, everything is money, because the people have to go so far to the bar or far places to catch fish, and when they bring they don't bring an amount because they sold everything to the company. So when they come is just a small amount they bring along and if you need a fish, you have to buy it.

Many interview participants, like Eduardo and Ray, indicated that prior to intensified commercialization of the fisheries, fish were commonly given away by returning fishers. The stable market for fish in the lagoon has changed this distribution pattern. Now fishers often return home with only enough for their immediate family and sometimes close neighbours and friends. Fish that were given away in the past are now sold in the community, although at a price that is somewhat lower than that offered by the processing plant. And the fish that are available in the community are often the ones rejected by the company because they are too small or the wrong type.

The situation in Orinoco is a bit different, because of the greater distance to the processing plant. There, availability of fish for local consumption appears to fluctuate with the presence of the *Sunrise*, the boat that comes to the lagoon to buy fish from the community. Orinoco resident Colestra explained:

> It affect, because when the boat is here buying we cannot get food.... You hear some of us in the community say, well the boat is here now, we sure we not going to be able to get a fish. If we don't have our husband fishing or our son is fishing, it come very hard to get a piece of fish.

When the *Sunrise* is in Orinoco the situation is the same as in the other communities: fish are only given or sold to close family and friends and they tend to be those rejected for commercial use. At other times, fish are more difficult to sell, so they are more available locally.

Although fish can still be found in these three communities, they are not as widely available as they were in the past. Some believe that this has not had a major impact on the food supply, but others believe there has been an adverse effect.

Lesbia from Haulover sees a decline in the amount of fish available, but she does not view it as serious: "Plenty [of fish] right now, not plenty like first time though we still have enough to eat." Salomen from Orinoco expressed a similar view of the situation there: "I mean sometime it would be a little effect but some very small. Like only today I can't get a piece of fish, but tomorrow I have lots again."

Ella Shwartz of Kakabila holds a fairly extreme view on the subject:

> It soon done because the gill net too much, the fish small and big it killing out now we all going to dead.... So no food around here nothing. It is cassava and that no strength. Sometime it hard for beg fish, hard for beg meat.

Although Ella sees the situation as a little bleaker than most, she expressed the concerns of many people in these communities.

Samuel Hudson of Haulover explained how he believes declining availability of fish has affected people's diets:

> Because one of the things is people have been accustomed to a lot of fish here and now it come in to change the diet. It not the same, so you expect that the high price of the meat and the expense and the economical part here are very bad.... [The fish] are very scarce, so then... it difficult because the fish is much cheaper. So then it humbug your diet, because probably when you don't have fish to cook then you wait until probably evening to see if you can get a piece of fish to cook. So then immediately you lost meal.

Eduardo Tinkam noted a telling trend in the community:

> You hear people talking about they're not getting fish, and this was something you didn't hear before; people would always say, well, I'm tired of eating fish. Now people are saying, we just can't get fish.

### Decline in available fish

Although there was disagreement about the seriousness of the decline in fish populations, interviewees generally believed that fewer fish are available. The number of fish distributed in communities depends on a number of factors: whether the fish are too small or the wrong type for processing commercially; the location of the community in relation to the company; and the presence and use of local iceboxes provided by the company.

For example, Kakabila is much farther from the processing plant than Haulover. Depending on the size of the catch and where and when fish are caught, it may not be economical for fishers to deliver their product to the processing plant, in terms of the cost of fuel or the amount of time required. As a result, Kakabila fishers are more likely than Haulover fishers to bring fish home or sell them in the community of Pearl Lagoon than to sell to the plant.

Orinoco differs from both Haulover and Kakabila in that fish supply is only affected by commercialization when a boat is in the community to buy fish. Orinoco is significantly farther from the market than either of the other two communities; thus, when the processing company's boat is not present, fish are more likely to be available for consumption within the community.

These changing distribution patterns are seen by some in the area as having important consequences on the availability of food, especially protein. The situation is compounded by the increasing difficulty of catching fish with less-intensive techniques, such as hand lines, which would previously have provided a secure way of obtaining fish for their own use by most people in the community. Changing distribution patterns for lagoon products have an immediate impact on the well-being of those with less access to modern fishing gear. In effect, the decreasing access to fish in these communities, especially among the less affluent may be undermining the traditional social safety net to some extent by taking fish partially out of the system.

## Increasing social differentiation

Another result of increasing commercialization of the fishery is social differentiation. When asked directly about the difference between poor and rich people in the lagoon, most participants denied that there was one. Many responded that they were all equally poor, although most conceded that some people were a bit more affluent. In discussing the issue more indirectly, however, it was clear that some residents in the communities have more economic opportunities than others, because they have access to more sophisticated fishing gear such as motors and nets. Lesbia from Haulover explained the differences in the seabob shrimp fishery:

> Well some people think different, yes, because for instance, some people in the seabob catching who have motor and who have trawl net can make an amount of money, and who don't have can't, because you hardly could catch with the hand net.

Richard of Orinoco described a similar situation:

> Most people here don't have gill net. So in other word, who have gill net destroy the fish. They make money, and also keep down the man with the handline then, because he don't have any fish.

In addition, access to modern gear is perceived by some to have an effect on the way in which people believe the resources should be exploited. A Haulover woman explained:

> Usually you could see it during the time of shrimps.... The people who have a little bit more money you know. They have more access to having a motor and thing like that, and they would usually trawl in the lagoon which destroy the ecosystem. But... when you talk to them about it, them would say well that's not their problem, and they would take out the shrimps, because the shrimps is there to take out.

The woman suggested that other people in the community cannot do anything about this because "the people that have the money is who have the say." Marcus from Orinoco also saw a difference in attitude between those with modern fishing gear and those without:

> People with more gears and more money they... doesn't take in much consideration the way of exploiting it. They does do that to make money and to get richer and... say to hell with who stay behind you.

It is likely that the amount of resources available to people in the community has at least some effect on the way in which they believe the lagoon should be exploited.

Access to modern gear also increases the opportunities available to people. Ownership of a motor opens up the possibility of fishing in the ocean or traveling greater distances to more productive areas. Those with motors could trawl for seabob outside of the lagoon, something that was resented to some degree by those without motors who had to harvest this lucrative resource using a cast or drag net. Victor from Haulover explained:

> I see one day I did trawling with my little drag net... When I look some of the motor closer than them which walking [pulling a small trawl net by hand]. Them trawling some of them trawl closer than you. They real rough.

Victor's concern is that people with trawl nets and motors are making it increasingly difficult for those without to catch seabob. Also, although people with motors can fish in different locations than those without, they often choose to fish in the same locations, making it more difficult for the disadvantaged fishers.

While social differentiation is not particularly great, commercialization of the fisheries is clearly beginning to widen the gap between "haves" and "have-nots." Differences in people's abilities to exploit the fisheries resource, based on availability of capital, increase differences in the way people believe the resource should be used. Although it seems that people with access to modern equipment are inclined to exploit the resources as intensively as possible, others are more concerned about the long-term viability of the fisheries as a way of life in the community as a whole. In addition, there was clearly some resentment against those who are unconcerned about the future of the lagoon and are presently exploiting it as intensively as possible.

## Reaction to changes

Reactions in Haulover, Kakabila, and Orinoco to the changes occurring in the fisheries are varied. A segment of the population remains unconcerned about the possible effects of increasing commercialization; however, many people express concern about the future and are looking for ways to ensure the continued viability of this resource and the community's way of life. In the following sections, we examine various community views on how to deal with the changes in the use of the lagoon: limiting exploitation, limiting fishing by outsiders, and preventing wasteful practices.

### *Limits on exploitation*

When asked what could be done to protect lagoon resources, many interview participants suggested some type of ban (veda) on harvesting. Suggestions ranged from a 2-year ban on fishing in the lagoon to vedas on catching certain species, at certain times or in certain places. Regulation of the type of gear people can use was also suggested. Many people believed that catching juvenile or spawning fish was destructive and should be prevented. Participants often pointed out that although a veda of some kind would be the ideal, it would not be possible unless alternative economic activities were available for people. Paul of Kakabila and Charles from Orinoco assessed the problem as follows:

> Paul: This Nicaragua them bad man, because through no work... in Nicaragua that's why the people have to fishing, because if they no do that, they no have no money for buy.

> Charles: When the time of the things [shrimp or fish season] come we have to make use of it, because if we don't make use of it, it pass and go out to sea and the big boats they steal it and then we don't have nothing, and then we have nothing else to do... to live off. Now if the government would bring in a working system inside the community for us then we can go ahead with that. But, well if it is not like that, we can't do nothing; we have to catch it.... [We have] nothing else to live off.

Many people have to exploit these resources to meet their needs, as there are very few economic alternatives. In addition, Charles' sentiment that "if we don't catch it, someone else will" is widespread, especially regarding shrimp. People generally want assurance that plans to conserve fish and shrimps at their expense are not going to be undermined by others exploiting the same resource at sea.

According to Lesbia, not only are fish and shrimps the most important source of income, but engaging in any other productive activity also depends first on start-up money from fishing:

> The most thing that we living off right now is the fishing, because if you don't have fish or shrimps to catch and sell then you can't buy nothing. Well really who plant still have little breadkind and a little rice and thing but still. Any way, think it Mr Mark, you need the fish and the shrimps because you have to sell to buy something. Maybe I want to plant a little beans right now but I don't have the money. I plan when he [her husband] go fishing I going to buy the beans [to plant]. Okay, so if no fish and no shrimps, what I going to live off?

As a result of these limitations, many participants felt that people were unlikely to abide by any conservation regulations unless the communities were consulted during the drafting of the regulations and unless alternative economic activities were available. The most important alternative was marketing agricultural produce; other suggestions included exploitation of previously ignored species in the lagoon, such as sardines, or the introduction of some form of ecotourism.

The people interviewed generally showed concern about preserving the lagoon resources and expressed a number of alternatives for accomplishing this goal. However, they also saw few economic alternatives to continued exploitation of these resources, and clearly felt they would be unable to accept measures that would prevent them from making a living. Many stressed the importance of coming up with alternative productive activities to decrease pressure on the lagoon.

### Limits on outsiders

Interview participants also expressed concern about excessive exploitation by small groups of people, especially from outside the lagoon. Many people indicated that they did not like people from Bluefields using the lagoon, but that it would be acceptable provided that these people did not overexploit. Respondents generally felt that everyone has a right to make a living; as Orinoco resident Salmon said, "Garifuna people sense that everybody have to eat a bread." In addition, most people expressed concern about boats coming from Bluefields with 30 nets whereas lagoon residents tend to use four or five. This use of a large number of nets is seen by community members as interfering with the ability of local people to catch fish.

Bernadino a fisher from Kakabila related one incident and described how it was handled by local fishers:

> Well here we had a problem, not all the people from Bluefields but we had one guy by the name of Putku, he had two boat here they name *Vanessa 1* and *Vanessa 2*.... These two boat each one of them had 16 gill nets and they went to Hog Key and they put out their 16.... We fishermen from in Pearl Lagoon, Haulover, Kakabila, Brown Bank we can't catch fish.... It's so much net they can't manage it and the fish spoil and dump it.... This year we tell the old man Putku, if you are going to do this, you better get from here immediately because we people from inside the basin of fishermen, we don't do this and we never permit no one to do this, because this is not right.

Resistance to the use of the lagoon by people from Bluefields was reserved mostly for those perceived to be overexploiting, wasting fish, or using methods that threatened lagoon residents' ability to make a living. One community member,

Eduardo, suggested that this was not entirely true:

> Now we could think about people from Bluefields coming to fish, and one of the things we could say to people is, don't use that type of method, don't use this amount of nets. But these people logically are going to say, if I don't use this amount of nets, maybe I only bring four nets it wouldn't be rentable [economically viable] for me, so then I just won't come. So its like saying, its better for them not to come.

Clearly there is resentment among lagoon people against those who come from Bluefields or elsewhere to overexploit lagoon resources. However, local people will tolerate people from outside who use the resources in what is perceived to be a responsible way.

Some respondents were worried that people come to the lagoon because they have already destroyed their own resources. In the words of Samuel Hudson from Haulover:

> One of the situations we find is that we are looking on a very serious situation that people is coming from Bluefields to fish in Pearl Lagoon and we ask the question why. It's because Bluefields doesn't have anything? And we say, why Bluefields don't have anything, is strictly because they didn't take care of what they have.
>
> So now we are looking on also an experience that passed with different Honduranian boats that come down from Honduras and fish here in Nicaragua. So we ask why Honduranian boats come to Nicaragua? It's strictly because you destroy what you have, and we also have the Colombian, also the Mexicans, the Panamanians, the Jamaicans come here because nothing over there.
>
> So we say then we are looking on Bluefields as another community that destroy what they have and now come from Bluefields to destroy what we have. So we said now where would we go.... So we said ok, if the Bluefields fishermen would like to come they would have to abide under the law that the community set. If we said, you're going to use two net, you use two net. If we said, you're going to use five inches mesh, then you will use that. Still after considering that we all is from the region, consider that we all need to eat, but also we need understand that all need to take care of what we have.

Samuel exemplified a degree of awareness in the communities that people from other places have destroyed their own natural resources, compounded by a concern that they not do the same in Pearl Lagoon.

**88**

### Avoiding wasteful practices

There was a strong desire among many interview participants to minimize what is perceived as wasteful and destructive practices. For example, they want to police the operations of the fish processing plant. Many mentioned the distribution of fine mesh (6-cm) gill nets by the company was unacceptable. Herman explained:

> Interviewer: So mostly the company bring in gill net?
>
> Herman: Yes, and well, afterwards when this become popular because we see that well, these things catch fish, catch fish and catch fish and catch fish until finally done in with the fish. So it is better now that we have to realize, I get to realize that it is better we didn't got gill net. We [would] have lots of fish in this lagoon. So to that day, now that gill net becoming a problem, because... in the early part of last year a guy came to bar point [the fish plant] with some nets. Special nets with fine meshes destroying all the little fishes which doesn't go up to get to know marketing size and destroy the whole lagoon.
>
> Interviewer: How big was the mesh?
>
> Herman: The mesh was about 2.5 inches maybe 2 inch almost shrimps could get catch in that?
>
> Interviewer: Yea?
>
> Herman: Yes, and we protest from the union. We wrote a letter to this man telling him we are not agree with this, and we would like him not to distribute these nets to no fishermen, and not to use them in the lagoon. It wasn't too effective, it didn't give us no answer, and finally we had to meet. In meetings is where we get to convince... the company that they mustn't do that. They said they would take away all these nets and burn them. Up to the actuality that it doesn't happen, because who got the net? Them still have them because here they have some, and who have them mighten know the damage. But you know who know? Those who give the net, because they come from another country, done wreck up everything and now come to finish with us.

Herman illustrates an awareness among fishers of the limitations of fisheries resources as well as some ability of the fishers to organize themselves to change company policies that they believe threaten the resource. In addition, it once again reiterates the concern expressed by Samuel that people from outside have destroyed their own resources and could potentially do the same in Pearl Lagoon.

Another concerns that was mentioned often is the need for people to tend their gill nets adequately. Colestra of Orinoco said:

> You know why it [the gill net] destroy the fish, is the mens them they are not capacitated to say attend your net in the way that you should attend your net. You go put that thing out whole night until next day, you go some time you don't even get a good fish to sell. What you get is spoiled fish, so what you going to with it? Just throw it away.

Because of the high water temperature, it is necessary for fishers to remove fish from their nets frequently to prevent spoilage. This often does not occur for two reasons. First, some people do not understand the importance of regularly tending their nets. Second, and perhaps more important, it is often difficult for people to return to their nets because they are far from home, and staying near the nets is uncomfortable.

Richard from Orinoco suggests that the problem of fish spoilage is often the result of people using more gear than they can handle. He mentioned this problem, referring specifically to Bluefields fishers: "Them can't even handle the amount of nets they have so they just kill the fish and have lots of waste with spoiled fish." He argued that Bluefields fishers especially tend to have this problem because of the number of nets they use when they work in Pearl Lagoon.

Local people believe that this problem can be solved in several ways. First, when company boats like the *Sunrise* come to communities, they often accompany fishers to the fishing ground and provide a place for them to eat and sleep while they tend their gear. Second, the use of motors also makes travel to and from nets more practical, although also more expensive — requiring stable and consistent production.

Concern about wasteful practices and the limitations of fisheries resources were common. The protest against the use of small gill nets demonstrates some ability on the part of fishers to organize and influence the policies of commercial ventures, when they feel strongly about the issues.

## Conclusions

The increase in commercialization of the fisheries sector has had negative effects on traditional mechanisms for subsistence security. It has led to the depletion of fish stocks and a shift in exchange relations from those based on reciprocity and social obligation to market-based exchange. In addition, it has led to a decline in the other major subsistence activity, agriculture, as people increasingly focus on the cash economy associated with fishing. These changes are not considered particularly threatening by many in the communities, who embrace the opportunity to earn cash through fishing. Others are more cautious, however, perceiving a potential threat to their subsistence security if the fisheries are not properly managed and market activities are not diversified into other areas such as agriculture.

Although the shift of focus into cash activities like fishing is normal in these communities, in this case, it also plays an important role in eroding the viability of the subsistence economy. Also, the shift is gradually becoming irreversible, as young people increasingly avoid the farm and women, who have traditionally been central to maintaining subsistence agriculture, often no longer participate in farming.

Moreover, the encroachment of the agricultural frontier on community lands means traditional farming areas for these communities may not be available in the future. This danger was identified over 20 years ago by Nietschmann (1973) and Cattle (1976) and has renewed significance in the post-Sandinista years, as the agricultural frontier is once again expanding due to cessation of hostilities in the region. In addition, the rollback of land reforms in the rest of Nicaragua is adding to the number of people looking for land. The encroachment of the agricultural frontier has been less a problem in Kakabila, as most families still maintain their subsistence plots near the community. In Haulover and Orinoco, agricultural production for consumption appears to be declining more significantly, and people are increasingly purchasing their food.

Exploitation of the fisheries has intensified both in terms of the number of people involved and the techniques used. According to most people interviewed, the result has been a decline in the number of fish in the lagoon. Although lagoon fish resources are being exploited more intensively for the market, people believe that it is taking more and more effort in terms of both time and gear to catch the same number of fish. Traditional techniques that are universally accessible, like fishing with a hand line, are becoming less reliable. This has had an impact, both on women fishers in Orinoco who traditionally have fished commercially using hand lines and on those lacking gear who sometimes fish with a hand line for household consumption or for sale.

Changes have also occurred in fish distribution patterns in these communities. Whereas fish were once widely distributed by fishers for free or at low cost, it is becoming increasingly difficult for some people in the communities to obtain this dietary staple. Although some fishers still give fish to close friends and family in their communities, increasingly fish tend to be sold, thus eroding traditional patterns of reciprocity based on social obligation. Apparent decreases in stock make less-intensive fishing techniques, which are used to supplement domestic consumption, less productive.

Finally, there has been an increase in social differentiation based on the capital available to various fishers. This has resulted in differing opinions in the communities about the way lagoon production should be exploited. Some people with access to modern gear are reported to be exploiting the lagoon as intensively as possible, which has caused some concern and resentment among others who fear that lagoon resources may be depleted too quickly.

## Annex 1: Interview guide 1

*Demographic information: (name, age, occupation, ethnicity)*

### I.   Fish reproduction

1.   How do fish and shrimps reproduce?
2.   Where do they reproduce?
3.   What conditions do they need to reproduce?

### II.   Traditional fishing grounds around this community

1.   What are the traditional fishing grounds here?
2.   What types of fishes are caught in these grounds?
3.   What types of gear do people use on these grounds?
4.   Are these grounds used as they have been used before? If not, why not?

### III.   Traditional practices of the community for the protection of natural resources

1.   What are the traditional practices of the people here for the protection of their natural resources?
2.   Which laws are still in practice and which are not? Why not?
3.   Who made these laws? Who enforced them? Would you like these laws to come back?
4.   What do you believe could help in protecting the natural resources?
5.   What law would you suggest for a management plan?
6.   What has autonomy done to help? How could it be better?
7.   What have organizations done to help? How could it be better?
8.   How does your community influence the government concerning fishing issues?

### IV.   Water quality

1.   What are the reasons for the color of the water in the lagoon? ·
2.   What months of the year is the water saltiest and warmest?
3.   What causes the water to be saline and warm?
4.   Has the top of the water and the bottom the same salines and warmness?
5.   What part of the lagoon is saltiest?
6.   Do you think the salines and warmness of the water have to do with the presence of fishes and shrimps in the lagoon?
7.   What months of the year do you consider dry season?
8.   What months is rainy season?
9.   What kind of breeze blows during the year?
10.   Do you consider the lagoon a place for fish to grow or do you consider it a place to fish?

### V.   Factories, foreign fishing

1.   What effect do you think the factories and foreign fishing have on your community?
2.   Has your community made any demands on the factories? What and how?
3.   How do you solve problems of foreign fishers?

### VI.   Training

1.   How did you come to manage all the information you know around natural resources?

## Annex 2: Interview guide 2

*Demographic information: (occupations: you and family, ethnicity [what group do you see yourself as], location [where do you live, where did you live], age)*

### I. Lagoon production for subsistence versus market

1. Have you always been able to sell lagoon production to the fabrics (for out)?
2. Do you think the union ice plant is a good alternative to the fabric?
3. Does more or less lagoon production go for out now than in the past? Does that effect the amount of fish people have to eat?
4. Do you remember when the gill net was introduced? What do you feel the effects of it have been? On you? On the community? On the fish? Are there any other inventions that have effected fishing?
5. Has the way fish is distributed in the community changed over time? Why?
6. When people distribute fish in the community, do they charge for it? Do they get the same price as the fabric gives? Has it always been this way?
7. Do people give fish away to family, friends or neighbors at any time? Did they use to?
8. Is there as much fish available today for people to eat as there used to be? Why or why not?
9. Is there enough fish for people to eat?
10. Do people feel it is all right for people from Bluefields to come fish or catch shrimps in the lagoon? Who do you think should be aloud to fish or catch shrimps here? Who do you think owns the lagoon production or is responsible for it?
11. Can the owner or care taker sell there rights to others? If yes: how, and what would it mean for the community?

### II. Importance of the resource for different groups

1. Has lagoon production become more or less important to your community than it was when you were young?
2. The lagoon production is important for making money in this community. Is it also important to the community in other ways?
3. Do people in the community agree about the way to use the lagoon production or do people have different ideas? What are they?
4. Do young people and old people feel the same about the way to use the lagoon production and other natural resources?
5. Do richer people and poorer people feel the same about the way to use the lagoon production and other natural resources?
6. Do people in the community feel different about how to treat natural resources than other communities in the lagoon?
7. Do people in the communities feel different about how to treat the resources than people from outside?
8. What would this community be like if the lagoon production was finished?

**III.**    **Effects of change in fishing on community members**

1.    Have changes in the way lagoon production is used affected different people in the community differently? Men, women, poor people versus richer people, children?
2.    Do some people get more benefit from the lagoon production than others? Who? Why?
3.    Have the changes in the lagoon production effected how the community deals with people from out? Fabric owners? Government? Groups from outside?

**IV.**    **Solving the communities' problems**

1.    Who has been responsible for making laws/rules about lagoon production in the past and now? What is the role of the community?
2.    Who has been responsible for enforcing lagoon production laws/rules in the past and now? What is the role of the community?
3.    What are the biggest problems facing the community with regard to the lagoon production?
4.    What things should be done to solve these problems? Who should be doing these things?
5.    Are there any things that hinder this type of solution?
6.    What would help overcome these problems?

**V.**    **Role of men and women in the communities**

1.    Are there different roles for men and women in the community?
2.    Do women work on the farm? Did they used to? Why did that change?
3.    If women used to work on the farm and don't now, who has taken over that work? Do people do as much farming as they used to in the old days? Why or why not?
4.    Do women take part in lagoon production? Did they used to? Why did that change?
5.    What other things do women do to make money or help contribute to the household/family?
6.    What do you think the effect of the changing role of women has been on the community?
7.    How do you feel about these changes?

## Annex 3: Participants in first set of interviews

| Name | Community | Sex | Age | Ethnicity | Occupation(s) |
|------|-----------|-----|-----|-----------|---------------|
| Anonymous | Haulover | M | ? | ? | Fisher |
| Anonymous | Haulover | M | ? | ? | Community leader<br>Fisher |
| Anonymous | Haulover | M | ? | ? | Fisher |
| Mackinley | Haulover | M | 85 | Miskitu | Farmer*<br>Community leader*<br>Fisher*<br>Businessman* |
| Gretal | Orinoco | F | 41 | Garifuna | Fisher<br>Farmer<br>Hospedaje operator |
| Anonymous | Orinoco | F | ? | Garifuna | Fisher |
| Lorenza | Orinoco | F | ? | Garifuna | Fisher |
| Charles | Orinoco | M | 54 | Creole | Fisher<br>Farmer<br>Forestry |
| Hosario | Orinoco | M | ? | Garifuna | Fisher |
| Melida | Orinoco | F | 63 | Garifuna | Fisher |
| Bernadino | Kakabila | M | 44 | Miskitu | Fisher<br>Farmer<br>Community leader |
| Paul | Kakabila | M | 30 | Miskitu | Fisher<br>Farmer |
| Herman | Kakabila | M | 47 | ? | Fisher<br>Farmer |
| Winston | Kakabila | M | 23 | Miskitu | Fisher<br>Farmer |
| Ella | Kakabila | F | 60? | Miskitu | Fisher<br>Farmer<br>Midwife |

Note: ? Indicates that the information was not available. In Haulover, interviewers did not specifically ask for demographic information.
* The participant is not currently involved in this activity.

## Annex 4: Participants in the second set of interviews

| Name | Community | Sex | Age | Ethnicity | Occupation(s) |
|---|---|---|---|---|---|
| Ortego | Haulover | M | 42 | Miskitu/Creole | Fisher<br>Mason<br>Carpenter |
| Samuel | Haulover | M | 50 | Miskitu/Creole | Fisher<br>Lay pastor<br>Mason*<br>Mechanic* |
| Eduardo | Haulover | M | 50 | Miskitu/Creole | CAMPlab communal investigator<br>Pastor<br>Farmer<br>Fisher*<br>Teacher* |
| Anonymous | Haulover | F | Late 20s | Creole | Student<br>Teacher* |
| Victor | Haulover | M | 35 | Creole | Fisher<br>Farmer |
| Lesbia | Haulover | F | 27 | Creole | Washing<br>Baking<br>Processing plant* |
| Mackinley | Haulover | M | 85 | Miskitu | Farmer*<br>Community leader*<br>Fisher*<br>Businessman* |
| Salomen | Orinoco | M | 54 | Garifuna | Teacher<br>Fisher<br>Farmer |
| Colestra | Orinoco | F | 37 | Garifuna | Fisher (shrimp)<br>Farmer |
| Marcus | Orinoco | M | 41 | Garifuna | Fisher<br>Refrigeration technician* |

| Bonifacio | Orinoco | M | 42 | Garifuna | CAMPlab communal investigator Teacher* |
|-----------|---------|---|----|----------|------------|
| Albert | Orinoco | M | 29 | Garifuna | Fisher Farmer* |
| Richard | Orinoco | M | 20 | Garifuna | Fisher Farmer |
| Bernadino | Kakabila | M | 44 | Miskitu | Fisher Farmer Community leader |
| Ray | Kakabila | M | 40 | Miskitu/Creole | CAMPlab communal investigator Forester Fisher* Farmer |
| Herman | Kakabila | M | 47 | ? | Fisher Farmer |
| Winston | Kakabila | M | 23 | Miskitu | Fisher Farmer |
| Lorna | Kakabila | F | 40 | Miskitu | Teacher |

Note: ? Indicates that the information was not available.
* The participant is not currently involved in this activity.

# V

# CAMPlab: THE COASTAL AREA MONITORING PROJECT AND LABORATORY

Photo: Mark Jamieson

# 5.    CAMPlab: THE COASTAL AREA MONITORING PROJECT AND LABORATORY

*Patrick Christie, Bertha Simmons, Noreen White*

In the preceding chapters, we provided an overview of the people and resources of the Pearl Lagoon basin with emphasis on local perceptions and experiences related to changes in resource availability and the ways in which people have tried to deal with these changes. We have seen that responses to the ups and downs in fish stocks and marketing opportunities have been felt at both the individual and collective levels. One of the collective responses has been a participatory action research (PAR) project called Coastal Area Monitoring Project or CAMP, which was set up in 1993. (When the project took over the management of a local fisheries laboratory, it became known as CAMPlab.)

In this chapter, we describe how CAMPlab evolved, the challenges it faced and is currently facing, and the ways it can address such challenges. We also present selected results from field studies conducted as part of the project, including participatory monitoring of water, forest, and fishery resources; mapping of traditional land tenure; and the contribution of the project to the development of a natural resource management plan for the Pearl Lagoon basin. We describe the roles of people associated with CAMPlab and the endogenous and exogenous influences that shaped the realm of possibilities for the PAR process; a topic to which we return in chapter 7. This chapter builds on the data and detailed explanations of Christie (1999).

## Early stages: building a team, defining the agenda

Beginning in February 1993, Robert Rigby and Patrick Christie initiated CAMP with a small group of community members from Haulover and the town of Pearl Lagoon. At the time, Roberto was working as a technician at a marine laboratory in Haulover that conducted research on the lagoon's fishery and hydrology. Patrick was working toward his master's degree as an associate researcher with CIDCA. The initial 6 months of the project may be characterized as a phase of testing participatory methods for problem identification, which were subsequently evaluated (Christie 1993).

Between 6 May and 16 June 1993, six CAMP meetings were held. During the course of these meetings, a small group of 10–15 people — men and women from Haulover and Pearl Lagoon — reviewed the environmental problems they faced. Various means were used, such as small-group discussions, mapping, drawing, and ranking, to identify resource management problems and set priorities (Christie 1993). The absence of any legal, formal management framework for the area's natural resources was chosen as the most important local environmental issue that participants wished to address.

Although it may seem unorthodox to have identified the *lack* of a management regime as an environmental problem, within the context of an open-access system this, indeed, may be an underlying factor resulting in various, more tangible, problems such as overfishing or deforestation. In this case, participants preferred to try to resolve a fundamental problem, rather than a proximal issue. Participants felt that laws or rules would regulate resource use, especially in the prevailing climate of commercial expansion of the fishery and declining forest resources. A set of such of regulations is commonly referred to as a "management plan," a term that Patrick Christie introduced at this point and CAMPlab participants began to use. Community members felt that they had the right to participate in decisions that affected their livelihoods and communities. As a result of the 1988 Autonomy Law, they have a legal right, in coordination with the regional government in Bluefields, to participate in policymaking decisions.

Also in 1993, participatory environmental monitoring was initiated when the senior class of the secondary school in the town of Pearl Lagoon began monitoring a nearby river. Roberto and Patrick helped organize the fieldwork with the biology teacher and the 10 fifth-year students: eight from the town of Pearl Lagoon; the other two from Haulover. The students decided to monitor Mos Mos Creek using methods outlined in Mitchell and Stapp (1993). This creek was easily accessible and its water was used by a local ice-making plant. Local fishers and community residents consumed the ice; therefore, water-borne pathogens, including those that cause cholera, would pose a serious health risk in Pearl Lagoon.

The students analyzed their findings and presented them to the directors of the ice plant. They determined that the plant's water source contained fecal coliform levels (600 colonies per 100 mL) that were 60 times what is considered acceptable by the World Health Organization, an indication that the water was being contaminated by feces of warm-blooded animals (Table 6). As a result of the students' work, the plant directors vowed to chlorinate the water.

**102**

**Table 6. Results from monitoring the water of Mos Mos Creek, April and May 1993.[a]**

| Tests | Site 1: holding tank | Site 2: washing area | Site 3: intake area | Site 4: control |
|---|---|---|---|---|
| Dissolved oxygen (% saturation) | 42 | 89 | 88 | 88 |
| Fecal coliform count[b] (colonies/100 mL) ($n = 3$) | — | — | 600 | — |
| pH | 7.25 | 8.0 | 7.5 | 7.5 |
| BOD (mg/L) | 3.5 | 5.8 | 0.6 | 2.0 |
| Temperature difference between sites (°C) ($n = 1$) | 4 | 0 | 0 | 0 |
| Total phosphates (mg/L) | 0.3 | 0.5 | 0.2 | 0.1 |
| Nitrates (mg/L) ($n = 3$) | 0 | 0 | 0 | 0 |
| Turbidity (cm)[c] ($n = 1$) | — | 190 | 191 | 194 |
| Prorated water quality index (WQI)[d] | 72 | 82 | 81 | 92 |
| WQI range | Good | Good | Good | Excellent |

a. Averages are reported except for coliform count, which is highest value recorded; number of samples is two except where noted.
b. Fecal coliform count was only tested at site 3 due to limited broth supply and access to testing kit.
c. Measured using a Secchi disk; the disk could not be used in the water holding tank.
d. Total solids were not measured because an oven was not available; however, WQIs were calculated by prorating the index to the other eight tests.

Between June 1993 and January 1994, Patrick was out of the country and the project went through a period of quiescence. Planned activities, such as water monitoring and communal meetings, did not take place. However, encouraged by the results of the first phase, Roberto and Patrick submitted a proposal to IDRC for financial support. The proposal received a favourable review.

In January 1994, former participants were interviewed to find out whether they still had an interest in the project; most were willing to start again. Monthly meetings were resumed and, from April 1994 until November 1994, seven meetings were held, with attendance fluctuating between 6 and 17 people. At the first meeting, participants decided to continue the project, although they recognized that there were likely to be periods of activity and quiescence. Participants also expressed an interest in learning, first hand, about their environment. Subsequent meetings focused on planning the research and community-outreach events.

## Emergence of the CAMP committee

At this point, the small collection of interested people had begun to coalesce into a unique communal group. Its members identified with CAMP and began to refer to the group as a "CAMP committee." Its organization was based on a successful approach used in other community-based resource management programs. Although referred to by various names, these groups are typically open and consist of interested community members (White et al. 1994; Ferrer et al. 1996). Eventually, CAMP committees were also formed in other Pearl Lagoon communities, each made up of local people with an interest in natural resource management. The intention was that each CAMP committee would meet separately, but also with other committees and leaders to discuss their concerns about the environment, conduct investigations, and take action.

In 1994, field research became a main focus. Under the guidance of Roberto and Patrick, participants began to monitor the area's pine savannas because they felt that these ecosystems were a valuable and threatened resource. Forest surveys were conducted with farmers and students on three occasions at three different sites. From the information collected, the average circumference of pine trees in Pearl Lagoon's three savannas was determined (Fig. 4).

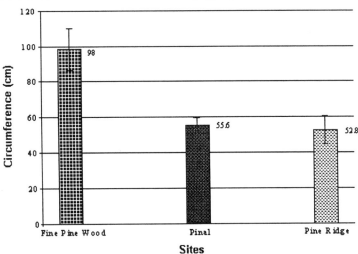

**Figure 4. Average circumference of *Pinus caribaea* in three savannas, 1994. Note: Error bars represent 95% confidence intervals.**

104

The general condition of two of these savannas was determined using a walk-through method, with sampling at various points along a transect (Table 7) (Christie 1999). From the information collected, it seemed that Fine Pine Wood had the most mature trees, whereas Pinal had been heavily affected by logging and repeated fires.

**Table 7. Summary information from walking transects.**

| | Fine Pine Wood, August 1994 (n = 19)[a] | Pinal, September 1994 (n = 20) |
|---|---|---|
| Habitat type (%)[b] | | |
| Pine/oak | 33 | 5 |
| Pine | 0 | 10 |
| Oak forest | 12 | 0 |
| Mixed thickets | 1 | 10 |
| Broken ridge[c] | 0 | 10 |
| Open grassland | 54 | 65 |
| Forest cover (%) | 13 | 5 |
| Number of stumps | 20 | 89 |
| Number of trees >50 cm in circumference | 153 | 28 |
| Number of trees >100 cm in circumference | 36 | 7 |
| Number of bird species | 11 | 5 |

a. Each sample point is a circle with a radius of 10 paces (about 10 m) and an area of about 314 m². 
b. Percentage coverage was calculated by treating each circle on the walking transect as a discrete sample. Some sample circles contained more than one habitat type. 
c. "Broken ridge" habitat refers to the types of trees and vegetation that grow on shallow ridges that run parallel to the sea shore (Nietschmann 1973). Many of the tree species are also found in the nearby rain forest.

In addition to providing the communities with useful general information about the area's natural resources, this activity also encouraged some students to consider new careers in resource management. Partly based on their brief experience with CAMP, three students and their biology teacher decided to pursue studies at two new universities in Bluefields, which offer courses in fisheries management, marine biology, and forestry management.

By August, the first full-time communal investigator from the town of Pearl Lagoon was hired. This phase of the project (called CAMP Phase I) was administered by CIDCA, who hired local people either full-time or part-time to live and conduct research in or near their community-of-origin. CAMP's communal investigators were employed full-time. Unfortunately, the Nicaragua's Ministry of Foreign Cooperation (MFC) and CIDCA, the project's implementing agency, delayed funding for over 1 year; therefore, during 1994 and early 1995, Roberto and Patrick were forced to cover basic project expenses and the communal investigator's salary.

Initially, CAMP was the only project dealing directly with resource management issues in Pearl Lagoon. However, in January 1994 another project with related objectives started. The Integrated Development of the Artisanal Fishery in Pearl Lagoon project (DIPAL) was a bilateral development project financed by the Dutch and Nicaraguan governments. The Ministry of Economy and Development's Department of Fisheries (MEDE-PESCA) was designated as the implementing agency. DIPAL's mission was to develop the fisheries sector through improved infrastructure and market networks, but within the framework of sustainable fisheries management (MEDE-PESCA 1993).

Until February 1995, various activities were undertaken by the CAMP team, but because of the delay in funding and the departure of some of the most active communal participants to study at the university, the process stopped. Without financial backing, the communal investigators lost direction and motivation.

> Mary: In November [1994] we had a meeting. In March [1995], there was a small meeting. At the meeting in March there was: Mr Edwin, Elmer, Noria, Roberto, Kenneth, Dirk, Johnny, and me. We planted trees after the meeting. We celebrate Mr Edwin's birthday.... Also had a January meeting at the school with a good amount of people. We evaluated things that we did in the past.
>
> We pressured the man who cut two pines in Fine Pine Wood. He was fined 60 cordobas. Fritz fined the man. We planted trees in front of the cemetery, the DIPAL office, and the park. We had a Christmas party in Fine Pine Wood. We had games and put up a sign board telling people not to cut the trees there. We made propaganda around Christmas in the churches, schools and person to person to not cut the pine trees in Fine Pine Wood.... During this time no research was done. [6 May 1995]

During one 3-month delay in funding, Kenneth, one of two communal investigators, decided to leave the project to return to farming. People reproached Kenneth for only being concerned about his salary.

> Johnny: With this project people need to make a sacrifice. He need to love what he is doing. So even if the salary don't reach, he will continue to work. This is always the problem with these projects. [6 June 1995]

By April 1995, the project had completely stopped in Haulover and Pearl Lagoon. Ray, the communal investigator in Kakabila, continued to work, although in a very limited capacity.

CAMP funds failed to arrive until May 1995, just before Patrick's return to the area for an 8-week field visit. Patrick and Roberto spoke with Kenneth and community participants about their interest in continuing CAMP and, once again, strong interest was an impetus for renewed activity.

The arrival of funding at this time allowed Kenneth to return to the project, and a third communal investigator, Bonifacio González, was hired to work in Orinoco. Forest monitoring recommenced and water monitoring was initiated in the lagoon. This activity was less participatory than water monitoring in Mos Mos Creek had been, mainly because of limited space in the boat, although youth accompanied Roberto on most sampling trips. The results are not presented here as this activity was less participatory and was discontinued due to its overlap with DIPAL's water monitoring program.

### Monitoring fish catches

At this point, local people expressed concern about what appeared to be a steady decline in fish yields. They claimed that the introduction of new, efficient gear (e.g., gill nets and trawlers) and the rapid expansion of fish-processing plants, which exported to international markets, were the main causes for this decline (see also chapters 3 and 4). The CAMP team decided to address this concern.

At a workshop, 15 members of the Haulover fishing cooperative were asked to identify the information that would be most useful to them in monitoring the condition of their fishery. It was decided that plotting catch per unit effort (CPUE) over time could elucidate general seasonal patterns and eventually reveal trends in fish and shrimp abundance (Saila and Roedel 1980; Sparre et al. 1989; Hilborn and Walters 1992).

After extensive discussion, and revisions, they designed a data form on which to record basic parameters that could be used to calculate CPUE, specifically, the number of pounds caught by genus for a particular outing. They also recorded the type and quantity of equipment used and the number of hours the gear was in the water. After the first year of monitoring, data on the number of spoiled fish were also collected. Only the data from July 1995 (when this activity was initiated) to November 1996 were analyzed as part of this preliminary effort.

Approximately 40 participants from Orinoco, Kakabila, Raitipura, Awas, Haulover, and the town of Pearl Lagoon recorded this information approximately weekly. The study focused on the southern lagoon fishery, which involved all of these communities except Orinoco. Because volunteers collected the data, the number of participant fishers and the number of days sampled per month varied. Fishers were given forms to fill out as needed. Some chose to fill them out almost every time they went out to fish, others less frequently, although data were recorded at least once each week. The communal investigators collected data sheets on a regular basis. In July 1995 and 1996 and November 1995 and 1996 a total of 19 different fishers from Kakabila, Haulover, and Awas were regularly sampled. This represents almost 20% of the "full-time" fishers of Pearl Lagoon (Bouwsma et al. 1997).

The people in the sample tended to be consistently devoted to fishing, as opposed to other activities, and were not novices participating in the fishery only when catches were large. Therefore, they probably represent some of the most effective fishers in the lagoon. The choice of fisher participants was not random. Only committed individuals willing to supply accurate data for long periods were asked to participate. On occasion, data were double checked against sales receipts by communal investigators to assess accuracy. Although this protocol might limit the potential to compare this study with others, the overriding purpose of the exercise was to monitor the fishery from year to year; thus, random sampling was sacrificed in favour of accuracy and commitment.

A preliminary review of the data indicated that gill nets were clearly the preferred gear for fin fish during the wet season, but that hooks and lines became the preferred gear as the water cleared during the dry season. Cast nets were still used most commonly for Penaeid shrimp, whereas trawl nets were increasingly common (and have remained important) for seabob shrimp (Vendeville 1990). There was insufficient data to conduct a meaningful study of hook and line or trawl net fisheries for this period, however.

The study was then focused on the two most common systems: gill nets for catching fin fish and cast nets for shrimp. To minimize possible errors due to the effectiveness of the gear, only 10-cm gill nets (the most common mesh size among participating fishers) were considered for this study. The length of gill nets was assumed to be relatively constant.

Local patterns of gear use and frequency of outings shaped the focus of this study on the most important time for the commercial fishery in the lagoon during the wet season. The peak of the coast's wet season is roughly from June to August, but conditions are wet for all months except March to May. Seasonal fluctuations in CPUE are likely related to the overall abundance of a particular species, but are also influenced by gear effectiveness (e.g., gill net effectiveness improves in the wet season).

To ensure that adequate data were available and to focus on the most commercially important species, fin fish species were grouped based on their seasonal presence in the lagoon. Snook (*Centropomus* spp.), jack (*Caranx hippos, Oligoplites saurus, Chloroscombus chrysurus*), mojarra (*Eugerres plumieri, Gerres cinereus*), whitemouth croaker (*Micropogonias furnieri*), and catfish (*Bagre marinus*) were analyzed jointly and referred to as the "wet-season assemblage." Because snook and shrimp are two of the most important target groups, they were also studied independently. Yield and effort data were recorded using Excel 5.0, categorized by gear type, site, or species as appropriate, then imported into Systat 5.2.1 for analysis and plotting. Although the data presented here were collected by local people, analysis was conducted by Patrick Christie. Workshops with community participants were held to analyze the data in a more participatory manner, but these were not very successful. The use of hand-held calculators to manipulate large amounts of data proved to be an insurmountable problem, and participants were not familiar enough with scientific methods.

Fish capture was investigated at two levels: the wider southern Pearl Lagoon (from Big Bight south to the southern end of Pearl Lagoon (see Fig. 2), and at one fishing site, called Hog Key. Focusing on a single fishing area was intended to minimize the possibility of bias introduced by the non-random search by fishers over a large area (Hilborn and Walters 1992). If only a large area was studied, it is possible that CPUE might seem to remain constant, whereas actual fish abundance may decline as fishers sequentially abandon fished-out grounds for more remote, unfished areas (Hilborn and Walters 1992).

Ideally, the choice of monitoring sites should have been based on a chart of catches and fishing efforts in the whole lagoon (Hilborn and Walter 1992, p. 177). However, this was not feasible due to the lack of data from most sites. According to catch records, 11 sites were used for fishing. Bar Mouth, Big Bight, Pigeon Key (the first key inside the lagoon), and Hog Key, were visited by Haulover and Kakabila fishers. Fishers from Raitipura and Awas fished mainly at Hog Key, Big Bight, Rocky Point (just west of Awas), Warban (to the northeast of Hog Key), Big Point (the first point north of Bar Mouth), and off shore from Awas.

The Hog Key fishing ground was chosen as a priority monitoring site based on its importance as a preferred fishing location for Kakabila fishers, and because, according to local accounts, fishers randomly distribute their nets within the area. Kakabila fishers' preference for Hog Key might suggest a higher CPUE for this site than for most areas, making it less representative of the wider lagoon. However, this was contradicted by the fact that Haulover fishers preferred Big Bight (25% of catch records), Bar Mouth (22% of catch records), and Pigeon Key (near the Bar Mouth, 27% of catch records) over Hog Key (5% of catch records) in 1996. Fishing site selection is likely to be influenced by unknown social factors other than fish abundance and proximity.

Cast net shrimping by Haulover and Kakabila fishers was focused at Big Bight, Bar Mouth, and Hog Key. For 1995, 63% of the shrimp records were from Hog Key and all were from Kakabila fishers. In 1996, 77% of the shrimp catch records were from Big Bight and Bar Mouth sites and all were from Haulover fishers. It is not clear if Kakabila fishers did not capture shrimp in 1996 or, more likely, if these activities were not recorded.

## Catch per unit effort for the southern Pearl Lagoon fishery

Box plots were used to display the CPUE data that were collected. Theses charts (Systat 1992, p. 180) "provide a simple graphic summary of a batch of data. The median of the batch is marked by the center horizontal line. The lower and upper hinges comprise the edges of the central box. The median splits the ordered batch of numbers in half, and the hinges split the remaining half in half again." (Systat 1992, p. 182). The ends of the "whiskers" of each box (the lines that look like error bars) extend to the last data point that is no more that 1.5 times greater or less than the absolute value of the difference between the upper and lower hinges of the rectangular box, measured from each hinge of the box. Asterisks represent values that fall outside the whiskers and circles represent "far outside values" that are at least three times the absolute value of the difference between the upper and lower hinges of the rectangular box, measured from the hinge of the box. In some cases, "far outside values" were not plotted because they would have made it difficult to read patterns in the graphs. These omitted data points affect the width of the plot's whiskers, however.

Figure 5 is a box plot of CPUE in kilograms per net per hour of fishing for the wet-season assemblage over time. We used these units rather than kilograms per boat or per day at sea, which is commonly reported when less information is available (Kapetsky 1981; Bernacsek 1984) because this provides a control for the fluctuations in number of nets used and hours fished that occur seasonally and between communities. Because the intention of this effort was to develop a monitoring mechanism to detect changes in the Pearl Lagoon fishery over time, this level of accuracy was more important than an ability to compare our data with other studies.

Figure 5 represents data from 522 fishing events. The location of the median line within each box indicates that the data are not very skewed, but the width of the whiskers for the October and November 1995 and July 1996 show that there is considerable variation in CPUE for these months. Median CPUE ranged from 0.3 to 1.4 kg/net per h, with the highest values in October and November 1995 and July 1996. These values are comparable with at least one other study that reports CPUE using gill nets in a Tanzanian estuary as 10.3 kg/net per day (Bernacsek 1984). With an average of 12 h in a fishing day using gill nets, the daily CPUE for Pearl Lagoon would range from 3.6 to 16.8 kg/net.

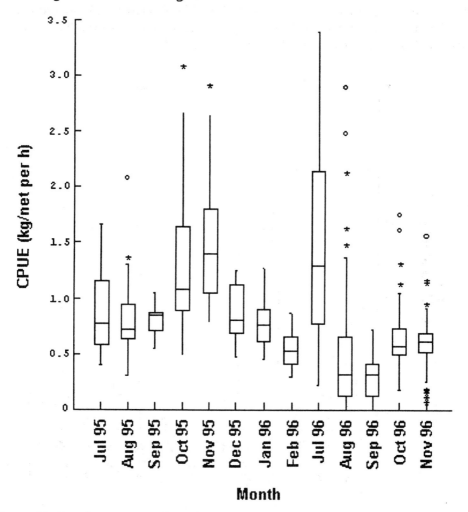

**Figure 5. Catch per unit effort for the wet-season assemblage in southern Pearl Lagoon (*n* = 522).**

Note: See text for explanation of symbols. Eight data points from July 1996 ranging in value from 6.3 to 10.5 kg/net per h and two data points from October 1996 (4.1 and 4.5 kg/net per h) are not displayed in this plot.

Peak 1996 commercial sales for these species, which corresponded to peak CPUE, were in July (49 816 kg), October (26 221 kg), and November (56 189 kg). The abundance during the wet season corroborates a study by Stoner (1986) who hypothesized that peak fish abundance corresponds to peaks in water column productivity (i.e., dinoflagellate standing crop and macro-zooplankton) and input of detritus.

When data from July to November were pooled and compared, an analysis of variance revealed no significant difference in overall mean CPUE for 1995 and 1996 ($F$ [variance ratio] = 0.14, df = 1, $P$ = 0.705). However, if data from July 1995 and 1996 were excluded, catches were generally lower in 1996 than 1995 for the remaining months ($F$ = 79.98, df = 1, $P \pounds 0.0005$).

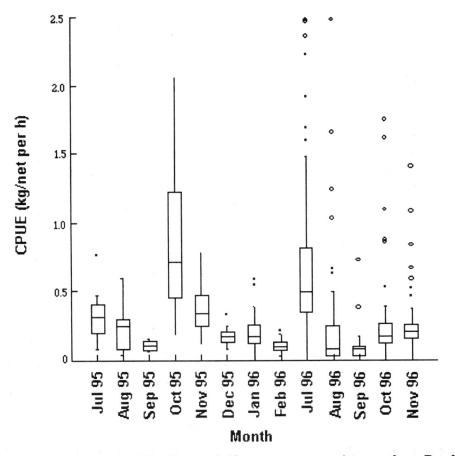

**Figure 6. Catch per unit effort for snook (*Centropomus* spp.) in southern Pearl Lagoon (*n* = 522).**

Note: Eight data points from July 1996 (ranging in value from 3.5 to 6.8 kg/net per h) and one data point from October 1996 (4.0 kg/net per h) are not displayed.

Snook catches from the same 522 fishing events were plotted separately (Fig. 6). Peaks in snook CPUE do not occur during the same months each year. The highest CPUEs were in October 1995 and July 1996, a result that was consistent with DIPAL's data on seasonal presence of snook in the lagoon (DIPAL 1996b). The general shape of the plot is relatively consistent for the 2 years with declining CPUE from July to September and an increase in October. Analysis of variance showed no significant difference in the pooled means for the overlapping months of 1995 and 1996 ($F = 1.451$, df $= 1$, $P = 0.229$). However, when data from July 1995 and 1996 were excluded, catches generally declined for the remaining months (August to November) in both years ($F = 8.820$, df $= 1$, $P = 0.003$).

The general shape of the data for snook is generally consistent from 1995 to 1996 and resembles the wet-season assemblage plot (Fig. 5). Furthermore, for July to November 1996, the shape of the CPUE plot is similar to that for the quantities sold commercially (Fig. 7); both peak in July and decrease to September. (The Pearson correlation coefficient for the relation between snook CPUE and snook sales was 0.8 [Bartlett chi-square statistic $= 2.6$, $P = 0.1$].) CPUE and fish sales should continue to be monitored and compared to determine whether the correlation between them continues. Their divergence might indicate that snook stocks are in decline while sales remain temporarily constant.

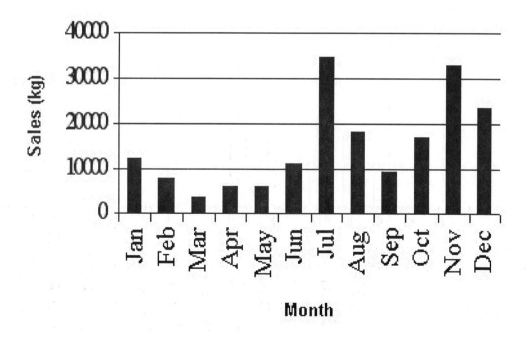

**Figure 7. Quantity of snook (*Centropomus* spp.) sold in 1996 (Bouwsma et al. 1997).**

Hog Key catches (Fig. 8) generally displayed less variability than the pooled southern Pearl Lagoon catches, a further reason for focusing on this site. However, the medians were more skewed than on other plots. November 1995 and July 1996 were peak months for the wet-season assemblage at this site. CPUE consistently increased from August to November in 1995 and 1996.

Overall, CPUE at Hog Key was not markedly higher than shown by the pooled figures for southern Pearl Lagoon. Therefore, its value as a monitoring site is not diminished. Furthermore, the shape of the CPUE graphs for the wet-season assemblage in the southern lagoon and at Hog Key is generally similar. Analysis of

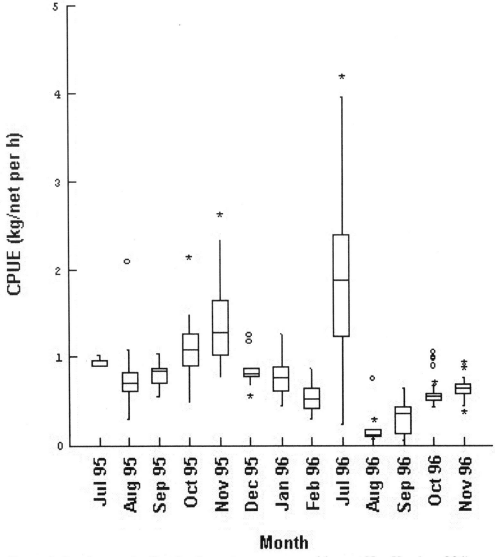

**Month**

**Figure 8. Catch per unit effort for the wet-season assemblage at Hog Key ($n = 324$).**

variance revealed no significant differences in the pooled means for corresponding months in 1995 and 1996 for Hog Key ($F = 1.737$, df $= 1$, $P = 0.188$). However, if data from July 1995 and 1996 are excluded, catches generally declined in the remaining months (August to November) sampled in both years ($F = 114.7$, df $= 1$, $P < 0.0005$).

Neither the graph shapes nor values for snook CPUE at Hog Key are consistent from 1995 to 1996 (Fig. 9). Such fluctuations may be the result of variable hydrologic conditions. A longer time frame is needed before we can comment on this variation.

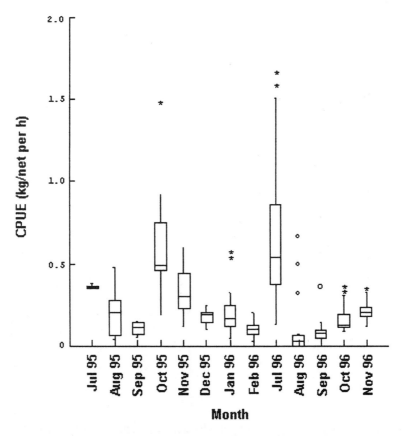

**Figure 9. Catch per unit effort for snook (*Centropomus* spp.) at Hog Key (*n* = 324).**

Note: One value of 2.6 kg/net per h is not displayed for July 1996.

CPUE values for shrimp also varied widely (Fig. 10), a phenomenon that is common for shrimp populations (Caddy 1989). In this case, a possible source of variability may have been the fact that most of the 1995 data were collected from Kakabila fishers, whereas the 1996 data were collected from Haulover fishers.

Most reports for Nicaragua and the Caribbean report shrimp CPUE only for the industrial, offshore fishery, thus making comparisons impossible (Morenza 1992; Martínez 1993; Sánchez and Cadima 1993; Ehrhardt and Sánchez 1995; Ehrhardt et al. 1995). The timing of the peak catch coincides with that reported in other studies for artisanal shrimping: August to October, as rains cause salinity in the lagoon to drop and adult shrimp enter the lagoon to reproduce (Lightburn et al. 1981). However, the data disagree with commercial landings, which peaked (5667 kg) in October 1996 (Bouwsma et al. 1997).

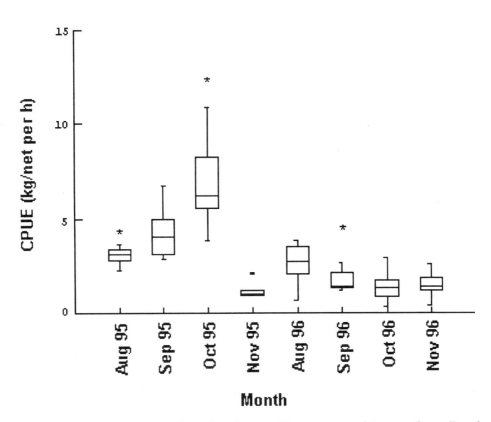

**Figure 10. Catch per unit effort for shrimp (*Penaeus* spp.) in southern Pearl Lagoon (*n* = 101).**

Note: In all cases fishers used only one cast net while fishing.

These results do not demonstrate a decline in CPUE from 1995 to 1996. However, based on local accounts, it is likely that CPUE has declined over the long term. A longer time frame is needed for reliable analysis of trends in fish and shrimp catches. The relative internal consistency of the data as well as consistency with external studies indicate that this monitoring activity is worth pursuing. The pattern for each plot shows that fin fish are generally most abundant in July, October, and November, a finding that agrees with Stoner (1986) and Yañez-Arancibia (1988), but the population varies from year to year in timing and number.

This data set contains at least some information from the early stages of the increase in fishing in Pearl Lagoon in 1996. Thus, it may be useful for monitoring the effects of the transformation of Pearl Lagoon's fishery. Similar CPUE analysis should be carried out in various areas over time. Also, demersal species (those living on the bottom of the water body) might be separated from pelagic species (those inhabiting the mid-depth range) within the wet-season assemblage to determine whether the relative abundance of omnivorous and less valuable species, such as catfish, is increasing as high-level and valuable carnivores such as snook are put under increasing fishing pressure.

Although the data collected during the fisheries monitoring are comparable to those of DIPAL, the possibility for comparisons with studies outside Pearl Lagoon is limited for three reasons. First, the amount of fisheries research conducted along the Caribbean coast of Central America is limited. Second, units of analysis are not standard. Third, the self-monitoring framework precludes random sampling of fishers. Therefore, fishery-monitoring efforts should be considered to be mainly of local use for determining the effects of transformation of resource use patterns.

Information obtained from monitoring fish catches for 17 months does not immediately suggest a management strategy. Only long-term monitoring will demonstrate what is occurring in this fishery. Recommendations for management strategies arose out of consultations with fishing communities, as discussed below.

## The process matures and expands

Through most of 1995, the PAR process remained unstable, mainly as a result of financial and administrative problems. Although CAMP funds had arrived, CIDCA's Managua office released them only sporadically. At this time, CIDCA was a highly centralized agency with all accounting and administration done in Managua, and all bank accounts were strictly controlled by the Managua office. Monthly requests for funds were required, communication was difficult, and delays in the transfer of funds were common.

In April 1995, despite CAMP's administrative difficulties, IDRC expressed interest in supporting the project for a second phase. Based on suggestions from CAMP staff and participants, Roberto and Patrick prepared the CAMP Phase II proposal. At the same time, Norwegian Popular Aid (APN), the sponsors of a small fisheries laboratory where Roberto worked, were evaluating their efforts in the area. As part of its review, APN was considering transferring its laboratory to a Nicaraguan institution. After consultation with the communal leaders, the external consultant recommended better integration of the laboratory's work with the communities of Pearl Lagoon (Ryan 1995b). When the consultant asked the Haulover Communal Council members for their opinion, they asked APN to transfer the laboratory, equipment, boat, and annual budget to CIDCA for use by CAMP. Many of the most active members of the council were original participants in CAMP. Their request was approved in August 1995, and CAMPlab was borne although funds were not available until November.

The laboratory transfer process was not smooth and caused animosity between CIDCA and the Haulover Communal Council. Part of the ill will arose from the unilateral appointment of an administrative director for the laboratory, Oswaldo Morales, who joined CAMPlab in November 1995. Another problem was that DIPAL had attempted to prevent the transfer of the laboratory to CIDCA, because it wanted the building to house visiting scientists and students. Eventually, after much discussion, this issue was resolved and CAMPlab field activities resumed with additional resources.

By the second half of 1995, the project team was involved in monitoring forests, fish yields, and lagoon water; environmental education; and community discussions about a management plan for the Pearl Lagoon basin. Environmental education generally took the form of presentations by staff and participants at the local schools and communities and consisted of slide shows illustrating local issues and interactive visual aids. The monitoring itself was also a form of environmental education. Partly to resolve tensions with the Haulover Communal Council, APN initiated the formation of an intercommunal board to oversee the use of the laboratory. By December 1995, it was clear that the administrative side of CAMPlab was improving and that fieldwork was benefiting from the change.

CAMPlab communal committees were now established in six communities. A wide variety of sectors were represented in these committees, which included fishers, farmers, students, teachers, religious leaders, both men and women, and both youth and adults. These committees generally met on a monthly basis, with CAMPlab staff assisting each committee's steering group. They acted as planning groups for CAMPlab-related activities. The level of activity of these committees was related to the level of attention offered by the staff member and the level of member commitment to resource management issues.

## A growing team

This marks the end of the transition phase during which CAMPlab was transformed from a relatively small, resource-poor project with little institutional support into a medium-sized project with both resources and support. At this point, a capable field staff began to take shape. An ecologist joined the team in February 1996. When Kenneth Fox left to work as project coordinator for another development agency in early 1996, he was replaced by Eduardo Tinkam, a well-respected Haulover community leader. In April 1996, CIDCA appointed a new coordinator, Cristobal Medina, whose main task was to see that funds were effectively administered and that the project received regular supervision. At this point, the staff comprised seven people: three communal investigators, an ecologist, a coordinator of the technical team, a laboratory director, and a project coordinator.

In the second half of 1996, monitoring continued, but staff and participants also began to focus on environmental restoration. Reforestation was initiated in Haulover and Orinoco. In 1997, an important administrative reorganization took place within CIDCA. Most notably, on the advice of donor agencies and a recommendation from an external evaluation, CIDCA's administration became increasingly decentralized. Control of project funds shifted to the regional CIDCA offices. Also the centre of CIDCA operations was moved to Bilwi (Puerto Cabezas), a coastal city north of Pearl Lagoon, and the first coastal director was chosen. Although the decentralization process was destabilizing in the short term, it yielded significant benefits for CAMPlab.

Meanwhile, approval of CAMP Phase II funds was further delayed. Although IDRC had expressed interest in funding a second phase of CAMP in the spring of 1995 and had reviewed a draft proposal in November 1995, disbursements were postponed when the Ministry of Foreign Cooperation delayed the signing of the formal project agreement until October 1996. During much of 1996, therefore, CIDCA was forced to pay CAMPlab staff wages from its general funds. Even when the IDRC funds arrived, they were not immediately available for field use. In fact, funds for field activities (in addition to staff salaries) were not available until February 1997, an indication that CIDCA management was still centralized.

## Toward CAMPlab–DIPAL cooperation

By 1997, CAMPlab and DIPAL were focusing more and more on the development of an institutional framework for a management plan. After years of mistrust, CAMPlab personnel approached DIPAL to work toward collaboration. As a first step, the two projects jointly organized a large gathering of regional and local leaders in March 1997. At this meeting, a lagoon-wide Resource Management Committee was established, which was expected to play a pivotal role in the development and implementation of a management plan. Also in 1997, CAMPlab staff concentrated on analysis of research results. A workshop to examine the forest and fisheries data was held in January 1997 with nine community members from various towns.

Research results were reported to 18 leaders from various communities at the first intercommunal meeting in more than a year. The meeting offered participants the opportunity to voice their opinion of the project and plan the following year's activities. During this meeting, participants expressed their appreciation of the project's valuable, albeit inconsistent, attention to the communities and the area's resource issues. Most people felt that administrative problems had seriously impeded CAMPlab's ability to meet its goals. External evaluators attended this communal meeting as part of an extensive review of CAMP's activities up to March 1997 (Roustan and Robinson 1997).

Forestry and fisheries monitoring continued in 1997, but water monitoring was discontinued as it overlapped DIPAL's activities. By February 1997, a full-time social worker, Bertha Simmons, joined the staff to work on strengthening the communal groups and ongoing evaluation of the research process. In 1998, Bertha became the project coordinator; she was the only female on staff, all but one of whom were now from the coast. Recruitment of female staff was hindered by the 1997 coordinator's skepticism of women's abilities to conduct fieldwork. Furthermore, when community members were asked to suggest people to fill positions, men were invariably recommended and accepted.

Throughout 1997, CAMPlab had better financial and administrative support and became more active. Staff participated in a number of workshops designed to improve skills: geographic information systems, water monitoring methods, and dendrology. Forest monitoring continued at the pine savanna sites and was extended to two rainforest sites. Reforestation in the savanna was intensified near Haulover and sign boards discouraging burning were placed in prominent locations. The monitoring of Orinoco's reforestation project was carried out with communal participation. Of the 450 mahogany (*Swietenia macrophylla*) seedlings planted in 1996, 260 or 58% survived. Fish-catch monitoring continued. Water monitoring resumed, but now focused on local wells. A number of wells in Haulover were found to be contaminated with coliform bacteria and closed for human use.

In June 1997, staff began to work on contract with a new project called "General diagnostic of land tenure in indigenous communities of Nicaragua," which was directed by University of Texas researchers and implemented by the Central American and Caribbean Research Council (CACRC). This project involved documenting communal claims to land and land-use patterns as the first steps toward resolution of the coast's land tenure problems (CACRC 1996).

**120**

The link between CACRC and CAMPlab seemed mutually beneficial, as the resolution of land claims was related to the effective establishment of an integrated management plan that would include aquatic and terrestrial resources. Also, CACRC's methods involved local people in the mapping and documentation process and trained them in the use of a global positioning system. CACRC's directors were long-time CIDCA collaborators and recognized the benefits of working with a staff who already had a strong relationship with the communities. This undertaking eventually became the main focus of attention for CAMPlab staff during the last third of 1997.

University of Texas geographers produced maps that CAMPlab staff presented to each community for validation. The purpose was to begin a dialogue within and between communities about boundary disputes. Eventually, these maps proved very useful in the development of a management plan for Pearl Lagoon's natural resources.

## Focusing on the management plan

In September 1997, DIPAL staff presented a draft of their integrated management plan for the area's hydrobiological resources at a meeting of the Resource Management Committee; the plan was entitled *Plan de manejo integral para los recursos hidrobiológicos de la cuenca de Laguna de Perlas y la desembocadura del Río Grande*. Then, without giving the community an opportunity to review and comment on the plan (except for a brief meeting with a few community representatives), DIPAL presented the plan to the regional government and the minister of MEDE-PESCA for approval. Notably, neither CAMPlab staff nor community members were involved in this process. CAMPlab staff expressed resentment at not being involved in the preparation, or at least review, of the management plan, and were concerned that the communities would oppose the plan and lose interest in future resource management initiatives.

Community participants who attended the September meeting with DIPAL reportedly felt that their input had been ignored. From this point, relations between DIPAL and CAMPlab became more confrontational. DIPAL staff complained of CAMPlab's slower pace, while CAMPlab staff complained that communities were being marginalized by what they perceived as a nonparticipatory process. They felt it necessary to organize a review of the DIPAL management plan by community members; they translated the plan from Spanish into English and distributed it among the communities.

Between January and August 1998, CAMPlab staff met with each community to discuss the plan. During these meetings, it became apparent that the vast majority of residents were unaware of the plan's contents. As a result, CAMPlab staff and community participants decided to develop a separate integrated management plan from the perspective of the community and considering both aquatic and terrestrial systems (the DIPAL plan did not include terrestrial systems). This new plan was based on three primary sources of information: comments about the DIPAL plan; the collected field data on the area's forests, fisheries, land tenure, and land-use patterns; and a review of other management plans in Latin America.

A first draft was completed in December 1997 and was validated in another round of consultations in each community of the basin. In February 1998, an official presentation of the revised plan was attended by community members, the municipal major, the municipal council, a deputy of the national assembly, and representatives of various government and nongovernmental institutions in the region.

CAMPlab's management plan consisted of a general overview of the principal terrestrial and aquatic ecosystems surrounding Pearl Lagoon, a general description of the social context, and general regulations for use of the area's natural resources (see box for a summary). Three community members were chosen to present the plan, based on their language skills, familiarity with the document, and negotiating abilities. The plan was discussed openly and shortcomings were noted. Regional councilors, for example, requested that sanctions for rule violations be added. After this meeting, CAMPlab staff and community members met with regional council members to work out minor changes to the plan and to develop a strategy for its presentation at a regional council meeting.

> ### Integrated management plan for the natural resources of the Pearl Lagoon municipality
>
> The plan has five core chapters: Introduction, Geographic area, Description of the relevant management areas, Types of resource use and norms, and Suggestions. The Types of resource use and norms chapter is divided into five sections dealing with the pine and savanna area, the broadleaf forest, the lagoon, the three nautical miles artisanal fisheries zone, and the coastline.
>
> For each of these ecosystems, a summary description is given followed by a list of current resource and proposed resource uses. For example, the following norms are defined for the pine and savanna system.
>
> - The municipal authorities together with community members should establish nurseries for the reforestation of the pine savanna.
> - Every 3 years there should a controlled burning of the savanna and this should be done in February.
> - The Fine Pine Wood area should be declared a reserve.
> - The Pinal, Pine Ridge and Pine Wood Creek should be declared protected areas.

- It is forbidden to grant permission for the commercial exploitation of lumber in these areas.
- Following the approval of this plan, a 10-year moratorium will be declared on the use of lumber in general in the pine forests.
- Following this moratorium, only trees with a 50-cm diameter (measured at a height of 1.30 m) or more could be selected for cutting.
- The exploitation quota will not be higher than 70% of the total number of trees with a diameter larger than 50 cm.
- It must be guaranteed that the 30% remaining trees will cover the totality of the various pine areas previously identified.
- It is the responsibility of the lumber extractor to reforest the areas with a minimum of three seedlings per cut tree.
- All lumber cutting permits need the approval of the community leaders and the municipal council.
- Following the approval of this plan, the entities in charge of the control and supervision of resource use will be the Ministry of the Natural Resources and the Environment, the municipal council and the community leaders.
- It is forbidden to establish agricultural or livestock activities in the areas of Pinal, Fine Pine Wood, Pine Ridge and Pine Wood Creek.
- avoid forest fires, 15-foot circles should be maintained around the pine trees; these areas should be cleaned twice a year.

Source: Adapted from CIDCA–CAMPlab (1999); translated from Spanish by Ronnie Vernooy.

Regional council members reacted favourably to the plan but expressed the need to integrate the DIPAL and CAMPlab plans. To this end, CAMPlab staff members approached DIPAL to reach an agreement on how to proceed toward the development of a unified plan. With the appointment of a new DIPAL project coordinator, it appears that there was increased interest in this sort of collaboration, and a new, unified plan is expected to be approved by the regional council early in 2000. Then, the challenging task of implementation will follow.

## Conclusions

The ups and downs in the CAMPlab process, the results, and the experiences provide important insights into the practice of PAR, local resource management, and coastal area resource monitoring. Most important, this study demonstrates that it is possible to conduct participatory research that includes ecological information. Local people and outside facilitators can work together to collect basic information that will provide a foundation for management decisions. The process of involving local people in this research program raised their awareness about a variety of issues such as water quality, the condition of forests, the effects of fire and uncontrolled logging, and the usefulness of the collection, analysis, and management of data.

The data derived from this process are comparable and complementary to other studies. The water-quality data generally agree with Ryan's (1990) monitoring of Mos Mos Creek. The forest data agree with and build on the limited studies of pine savannas in the area. Taking into account the natural variability of the aquatic systems, the fisheries results are in agreement with those conducted by DIPAL (1996b) and others (Lightburn et al. 1981; Stoner 1986). The trends revealed within the short study period are generally internally consistent, a sign of methodologic validity. With refining, these techniques could prove useful in other PAR endeavours with similar goals.

The research process and outcomes had shortcoming as well. The dependence on external agents to assist in the collection and analysis of the data was a limitation. In addition, there were differences between interests of local people and standard practices for environmental monitoring. For example, during the fisheries analysis workshop, local people wanted to analyze their data by community, not by site or species. There is also a need to further improve local research capabilities. The data analysis carried out by local people using hand-held calculators would likely have been construed as overly simplistic and misguided. Therefore, two types of research may be necessary for effective and timely responses to resource management issues: local, participatory analysis responsive to local concerns and capacities and a more traditional scientifically-informed analysis to underpin or augment the local analysis. In some cases the same data may be analyzed using both approaches.

The output from the research has been put to immediate use in some instances (e.g., water monitoring), is being put to use in other instances (e.g., forestry monitoring), and has yet to be realized in other cases (e.g., fisheries monitoring). The local ice plant operators are aware that they must always purify the water when making ice, at least partly because the condition of the water source is publicly known. CAMPlab staff and participants are currently reforesting pine areas that have been deforested and are developing a local strategy for managing the savannas based at least partly on CAMPlab's research.

The fisheries data are of less immediate use, mainly because of the natural variability of fish populations and parameters that are monitored. However, local fishers have used their own records to monitor the amount of money that the fish purchasing plant owes them. In the past, there have been discrepancies over payments and amounts of fish sold to export companies, partly because fishers are often not paid immediately after turning over their catch and they have not kept accurate records. They have also expressed interest in a locally controlled system that will serve as an independent mechanism to validate the research conducted by government fisheries scientists, who they feel tend to favour commercial interests.

**124**

It is interesting that the use of the data mirrors the level of participation in the analysis. Local people were most involved in the analysis of the water-quality data, less involved in the analysis of forestry data, and least involved in the analysis of the fisheries data.

The project has succeeded, in a modest way, in developing some components of baseline information for an area where previously little was documented; it has also demonstrated that long-term, low-cost monitoring of valuable coastal ecosystems is possible. Suffice to say that to improve the quality of the work, more effort in developing and refining participatory environmental monitoring methods is needed.

As an unintended result, CAMPlab participants have reviewed reports produced by other traditional monitoring efforts (e.g., Ryan 1990) and have begun to interact with scientists who visit Pearl Lagoon. These face-to-face encounters go far toward bridging the gap that has traditionally divided scientists from nonscientists and increases the relevance of the scientific efforts.

In evaluating the efficacy of the CAMPlab process, the ability of local people to conduct a particular monitoring task should not be the sole, or even the main, focus of attention. Rather, the process by which one collects data, makes sense of information, and relates it to one's context is of greater importance. The fact that participants continued these activities in the absence of CAMPlab staff is an indication that at least some knowledge of the research process and curiosity about environmental problems are being internalized by local people.

It is also necessary to assess the process from the perspective of two-way exchanges. It is abundantly clear that CAMPlab staff learned more about the area's resources, resource issues, and people's values by conducting this research jointly with local people than independently as disengaged researchers. In this sense, participatory approaches represent a better way to conduct applied research.

At the beginning of 2000, it is clear that project evolution is a long process that has required considerable effort on the part of CAMPlab staff and Pearl Lagoon community members. The participatory research process was slowed considerably by a number of factors: inconsistent financial support, vertical administrative structures, and the complexity of the issue at hand. Moreover, as reviewed by Christie (1999), the current political climate in Nicaragua is not conducive to this kind of community-based processes.

Nonetheless, a number of positive, substantive outcomes should be noted. Most important, the Pearl Lagoon communities have been able to use CAMPlab as a vehicle for engaging in the challenges of resource management and triggering institutional changes, although admittedly at a slow pace. CAMPlab has also played a central role in the reorganization of CIDCA from a top-down, traditional research institution to one that is now much more horizontally organized and more closely aligned with the interests of Pearl Lagoon communities. Finally, a unified, coherent and promising natural resource management plan lies on the table awaiting endorsement by the regional council.

# VI

## WALKING A FINE LINE: THE DYNAMICS OF THE PARTICIPATORY ACTION RESEARCH PROCESS

Photo: Mark Jamieson

# 6.    WALKING A FINE LINE: THE DYNAMICS
## OF THE PARTICIPATORY ACTION RESEARCH PROCESS

*Patrick Christie*

In chapter 5 we described the evolution of the CAMPlab research and organizational process. In this chapter, we analyze the strengths and constraints of this process. To understand its viability — defined as efficacy and sustainability — we have to orient it within the complex regional and national sociopolitical context. Our goal is to show how the process resonated or conflicted with local peoples' aspirations and social norms. This, in turn, will help explain the project's ability to recruit and retain participants whose energies were vital to the whole process. The CAMPlab approach resonated at a number of levels with Pearl Lagoon residents. An important aspect relates to Costeño aspirations, and we, therefore, pay special attention to this.

## Historical context

Throughout the 20th century, Nicaraguans have struggled against the oppression of a brutal dictatorship and foreign interventions (Walker 1997; Gordon 1998). However, the Costeño struggle has been unique. Costeños have been striving for their right to participate in their own governance and to ensure the creation of a civil society that represents their diverse aspirations and social norms *within* the larger Nicaraguan society.

The coast is a place where indigenous and Mestizo societies have clashed repeatedly. Multinational enterprises have extracted natural resources from the region on a large scale, with the complicity of the government and the labour of local people (Gordon 1998). The Sandinista revolution represented a radical shift in Nicaraguan society resulting in widespread participation in political and social programs, but the coast, generally, did not share in this upwelling of democratization. Eventually, the coast became one of the main arenas of the Contra war that pitted neighbouring communities against one another and displaced thousands from their homes. Finally, realizing that neither military might nor development programs would stem the counter-revolution, the revolutionary government began a remarkable process of negotiation with the coastal communities that resulted in the Autonomy Law and the associated governing bodies.

The current "neo-liberal" government, with its interest in trade liberalization and with the aid of powerful international interests, is making a headlong dash to insert Nicaragua into the world market and to erase any telltale sign of the revolution. The rights promised by the Autonomy Law are only recognized out of political expediency; in practice, they are systematically eroded (Butler 1997; Gordon 1998). In the name of national progress, the coast, once again, is expected to provide the raw resources for this most recent political/economic scheme, a direct affront to the spirit of autonomy.

## Taking care of the natural resource base

As we described in chapter 5, beginning in 1993, CAMPlab provided a venue for community members to come together to discuss common problems. Based on their past experience, most felt that hardship would inevitably follow on the heals of uncontrolled resource exploitation.

In sharp contrast to the commonly-held misconception that poor people in developing countries are not good stewards of their resources, increasing numbers of studies document the commitment of these people to act as stewards of their resources (e.g., Shiva 1989). In the current case, they hoped that CAMPlab would provide a means to reach their goals.

> Interviewer: What motivates you to participate in CAMP?
>
> Johnny: To be very honest, (it is) the experience that I had toward natural resources as a fisherman. After seeing the disaster that we have in our forest and also the fishing area, it was always a dream to find some support where we could be able to find a solution to think about taking care of the natural resource.... So this is what really motivate me. Because if we doesn't make a real management plan (for) how to manage our situation, I think in a few years from now our Pearl Lagoon will be a disaster. [23 October 1994][1]
>
> Marnie: [B]eing a biology teacher, I feel like this make me get to know what it is to have these natural resource around, the importance of them. Now if this was to disappear or finish, then we fighting a next problem. So then one of the thing that motivate me is the love towards natural resources. [19 October 1994]

---

[1] All informant names are pseudonyms, and quotations are left in Creole English. Names of well-known coastal politicians have not been changed.

These values come from a variety of sources, including direct experience with the environment and institutions such as the family and the church. For example, Mary's concern for the environment seems to be rooted in life experiences that extend back to her childhood and are part of her religious life.

> Interviewer: How did you get interested in protecting the natural resources?

> Mary: My parents would talk about it. And, in church one time. Because we use to go to Fine Pine Wood and they [the ministers] would talk to us about the importance of it.... I did go one time when I was younger to Fine Pine Wood and they explain the relation between birds and trees. [19 October 1994]

Other community members have had the opportunity to observe, first hand, what has happened to the resources of other countries in Central America and the Caribbean, and they wish to avoid the same mistakes. Maintaining a viable source of income is undoubtedly also an important reason for taking care of the natural resource base.

## Insecurity and tensions

Generally, many Costeños do not seem to feel secure; they perceive their world as one of lost potential. In particular, they feel that the resources of the coast have been squandered and stolen. Their current feelings have a long history. Some individuals connect exploitation of the coast's natural resources by outsiders with the poverty conditions in their communities.

> Alvin Shorter: When I was a boy, almost 40 year ago, I remember boats taking big rafts of log out to the Bar. Ships taking logs from here out to the United States. This causes less benefit to our people and our schools. [1993 interview]

One elderly leader in Haulover, a successful shrimp fisher in his day, is concerned about the technological changes and the impact they have on his community.

> McKinley Tinkam: Now we have cast netters and the trawlers fighting for the shrimp. The trawlers are running the shrimp out since they disturb them. These new nets are knit to destroy. They don't let even the little shrimp to pass. It wasn't like that before. I use to only trawl outside the bar and with larger [sic] mesh nets. [28 March 1997]

As exporters introduce new fishing technology, most recently small trawl nets for shrimp, there is increasing competition for the remaining resources.

Another important issue is the change in ethnic composition of the coast's population. An age-old tension between ethnic groups is growing. As more Mestizos (commonly referred to as "Spaniards" by non-Mestizo Costeños) arrive on the coast, the resentment seems to be reaching a crisis point.

> McKinley Tinkam: This land issue is important. That if people from the Pacific keep coming and taking land there is going to be a revolution and a lot of fighting. [Haulover, 28 March 1997]

Differences in land-use patterns contribute to the tension between long-time coast residents and these recent arrivals. Recent arrivers' patterns of land-use, largely based on timber extraction and cattle ranching, are distinct from those of native Costeños. Frequently the land ends up in the hands of large landowners.

> Edwin Morris: There are 3000 hectares of land in Patch river. Who are we losing it to? The Spaniards! They cut down the land. They plant grass. Then sell it. They then make it bigger. But it's ours.... The Spaniards come and rip [saw] the lumber. And we say, "These Spaniards are good!" (laughter) They rip the lumber, but Kakabila is left poor. This has to stop! [Kakabila, 10 May 1994]

In some cases, recent arrivals lack an understanding of sustainable farming techniques that have been developed over generations.

> Rocky Point farmer: We have to protect the trees over the rivers. If we cut these trees then the river dries. The Spaniards cut the trees and then it dries. They cut the trees then plant grass.

> Tasbapauni elder: If you give the Spaniards a foot, they'll take a yard! They are going to put us into the sea!

> Kakabila farmer: They are taking over all the land. They cut plenty of trees.

At times, CAMPlab meetings were dominated by discussion concerning inter-ethnic tensions.

> La Fe resident: ...We have talked like this before. We have to unite ourselves and take action! If we start something, the Spaniards will keep off" [20 February 1997].

Over the course of the fieldwork, this subject was raised and discussed in at least four meetings. The fact that it was raised so frequently reflects the concern of Pearl

Lagoon residents over the converging effects of what they perceive to be a number of negative trends: a fishery that is under increasing pressure, the loss of communal land to landless peasants, and deforestation due to unsustainable forestry and agricultural practices.

Initially, it appeared that resentment against Mestizos was ubiquitous among Pearl Lagoon residents. Most local people felt threatened by these people who spoke a different language, had distinct customs, and moved in to occupy communal lands. Pearl Lagoon residents gave the impression that the relations between the ethnic groups were characterized by negative stereotyping. For example, a common preconception was that Mestizo newcomers were more apt than Pearl Lagoon residents to resort to violence to protect their land. However, this prevailing attitude was countered by an empathy for these people who are generally perceived as extremely poor and by a respect for their work ethic.

During individual and group validation interviews with both CAMPlab participants and CIDCA staff, residents showed mixed feelings about whether Mestizo newcomers presented a threat to Pearl Lagoon communities. Most interview participants would not ascribe their problems to the arrival of Mestizos on the coast, nor would they express ill-will toward the Mestizos as an ethnic group. For some, this may be an outcome of increasing contact between people, especially in the main cities on the coast. The inconsistency between what people said during CAMPlab meetings and during validation interviews highlights the complexity of this issue. As with many issues on the coast, political positions and ethnic identities are not absolute; rather they change with the historic context (Gordon 1998). Opinions concerning Mestizo newcomers and their role in Costeño society may differ across ethnic and class lines.

Ultimately, Pearl Lagoon residents were apt to lament their own shortsightedness and to hold accountable government leaders and policies that encouraged unsustainable exploitation of resources.

> Alvin Shorter: For instance, here on the Atlantic Coast, the forest is completely ruined. If we should think back, we could only blame our father and our forefather. If we should think back, we could only blame our past government. [1993 interview]

In fact, criticism of the government and elites was more consistent than the resentment toward Mestizo newcomers. Some realize that the current crisis is based on policies that are decades-old, going back to the Somoza dictatorship. These policies encouraged the expansion of agro-businesses on the Pacific coast and forced the migration of poor peasants to the Atlantic coast.

## Demanding accountability

Community members have begun to demand accountability from their leaders. There is a feeling that many political leaders, regardless of their political persuasions, tend to make decisions on behalf of the communities, without truly understanding their perspectives.

> Johnny McManus: It's not what... Ray Hooker [an influential coastal politician] want to tell me... but what I feel, and what I think, and what I live here on the Atlantic coast. Ray Hooker not a fisherman, he don't know what I feel. [16 June 1993]

At a meeting with regional leaders and government agency heads, one Pearl Lagoon resident expressed his frustration and demanded that government agencies charged with managing these natural resources collaborate with the communities.

> Marcelino Sambola, Orinoco fisher: We can forgive all the things that have been done in our area. We in the communities feel these things the most. Now (we) have no trees to make houses. I would like MARENA [Ministry of the Environment and Natural Resources] to respect the communities and their rights. In the future, we want organizations to work only with the participation of the communal leaders. [5 March 1997]

Although community members widely criticize government officials for their role in establishing current resource-use policies, they have not yet abandoned hope of forging a collaborative partnership.

> Interviewer: What are your goals for this project?

> Johnny: My goal for this project, is to see that we get this management plan put in practice, direct with the help from the regional and also the central government along with the community. [19 May 1994]

In this respect, participatory action research (PAR) resonated with the aspirations of the communities. The origin of CAMPlab, as a project that emerged with strong community participation, answered peoples' desire for a voice in these matters.

> Mary: CAMP is a project what begin with the people themselves. Just so... CAMP start with the farmers, the fishermen. [11 July 1995]

> William Hodgson: CAMP is the only organization that work with the people.... People should be involved in the research since they get deeper down into these things. [29 January 1998]

The action research tenet to share decision-making was embraced by participants.

> Interviewer: So then... how do you feel about the way that decisions have been made about the activities we do?

> Mary: I really feel like it's a good way, because people themself participate, people themself from the organization participate in elaborating them work. And nobody told them that, okay, we going to teach this, this, this. Something that was imposing on them. But by their free will each person get their responsibility. [19 October 1994]

When the CAMPlab process complied with this tenet, it was able to foster feelings of ownership among participants, a condition that is usually a goal of any community-based effort as it is likely to ensure sustainability. However, maintenance of a sense of local ownership and control over the process has always been complex. As Johnny remarked, although the process may produce useful outcomes, the creation of a sense of ownership emerges from negotiation that takes considerable time to develop and is influenced by entrenched social norms.

> Interviewer: What is the main accomplishment of CAMP?

> Johnny: It has done so much. Most important is to give the people the insight around the management plan. Also the water testing and the organization, the groups in the communities.

> Interviewer: What is the main problem?

> Johnny: It's not clear who CAMP belongs to: some believe it belongs to CIDCA, some believe it belongs to Canada, some believe it is for Patrick. Some say we have to wait for Patrick. But it doesn't have to be this way.... This is the custom here. There were never projects before with communal participation. [30 March 1997]

On a practical level, the resonance of the research process also depended on how well it met the daily needs of people. For example, the water-monitoring exercise coincided with people's interest in having well-educated community members and healthy living conditions. As might be expected, the people of Pearl Lagoon have hopes for their community and children that are common throughout the world: they want to live in a nurturing environment, and they want control over their lives. Some residents felt that, through their participation in CAMPlab, they could help make this aspiration a reality.

> Interviewer: What moves you to participate in CAMP?

Johnny: I think of myself and my children. I learned that other countries are out of forests, without sea products. I want to live in a clean community. I want my children to be prepared [educated] and to eat good food. [30 March 1997]

When CAMPlab was aligned with the interests and aspirations of the communal participants, it generated impressive levels of enthusiasm. Some participants displayed an almost missionary-like zeal for maintaining and spreading CAMPlab.

Interviewer: What is your role in CAMP?

Johnny: As one of the founder of the community of CAMP, I feel like I still love the organization because I love my community, I love myself. And I really am certain [that] with CAMP we can reach what goals we have for this community: preparing [educating] the people in the community to know what is taking place, coordinating with them that they could understand really what is happening to our natural resource. And the goal that I have for CAMP is to reach to a higher level that we could reach so that we could prepare our community and have our community completely involved in CAMP.... My role I feel like is to keep CAMP moving. As a native of this soil, as born on the Coast, and a citizen of Nicaragua, my responsibility is to see that CAMP never fail. To keep my shoulder [behind it] that CAMP may never disappear. [22 June 1995]

Interviewer: What is your goal now for CAMP?

Mary: I see CAMP born and grow. I would like to see CAMP to reach to be something big then. Become one of the movement that help to take care of the natural resources that we have. Something coming from people, not from a political work. [11 July 1995]

## Aspiring for "autonomy"

The CAMPlab PAR process is also related to wider political debates currently underway on the coast; most particularly the one related to autonomy. One of the most closely-held aspirations of many Costeños has been to realize what they perceive as autonomy: to achieve the right of Costeños to establish their own policymaking process.

Johnny Hodgson, coastal political leader: If it happen that we really get what you call the autonomy for the Coast, it's very good. Because the Atlantic Coast has been populated for more than a hundred years, [but] never be able to make a decision for itself.... We always have people from out who

take decision.... We cannot take decisions... through the centralized [system].
We hope we will get autonomy. [22 June 1995]

Many perceive this as the only way that the resources and the unique culture of the
coast will be maintained.

Interviewer: How do you feel about this autonomy?

Mary: I really feel that it is something. I just wish it would be regulated. [It's
the] only way that really going to save our culture and natural resources of
our area. [11 July 1995]

The concept of autonomy is necessarily associated with strong community rights as
the community is the geographic and political unit of most immediate importance
to most Costeños, who historically have been isolated from central or regional
government structures. Most Costeños want to maintain the rights of their
communities, and they look to the Autonomy Law as one means to do so. Proponents
of communal rights are not isolationist, however. To maintain communal rights,
they realize they must engage in a collaborative relationship with their government,
both regional and central, codified by the Autonomy Law.

Although Costeños may have backed the Autonomy Law as a means to guarding
their communal resource base, the law is not functioning as was originally intended.
Since the implementation details have never been developed, effectively preventing
the regional councils from asserting their authority, the process has devolved into a
chaotic political struggle. As a result, people are becoming increasingly cynical about
the prospects for real change, especially as political parties rally behind the cause of
autonomy, seemingly for their own political gain.

Johnny, a Haulover fisher: Another thing that I'm worried about is that the
party of the government is always talking about the Autonomy, but never
one come up and say what is the true Autonomy. What I see is that Autonomy
is being used as a tool. Each party come use it, since they know that people
want Autonomy. So each party come during the election, [but] after [the]
election is over, they just forget about that.... If we could really get Autonomy
for the Atlantic Coast, I think we could [do] a much better job taking care of
the natural resources. [22 June 1995]

Despite the fact that cynicism about the likelihood of implementation of the Autonomy
Law has grown, the ideals that it stands for remain attractive to Costeños. Regardless
of the status of the Autonomy Law, they continue to hope for what the law was
designed to ensure: well-educated citizens, a healthy resource base, and political
voice. As a program that has been shaped by communal members, the CAMPlab
process is associated with these aspirations.

Bertha: How does CAMP fit with Autonomy?

Gerry: Same thing with this education line. Getting people prepared. Putting this thing in people's head to demand things.... This is a good thing. Now people are more informed about these things. [24 March 1997]

Mary: Autonomy and CAMP is related. Both talk about taking care of the natural resources.

Johnny: CAMP *is* Autonomy. It is to be able to manage their own project. CAMP practically giving Autonomy to the community. [validation interview, 30 March 1997]

Interviewer: Does participatory research and natural resource management resonate with the struggle you mentioned?

Faran Dometz, regional councilor for Pearl Lagoon: Certainly. That's at the base of Autonomy. People realize that the Coast could become a desert.... Political power without an economic base is senseless. And people need to participate in this process of management of natural resources. [1 July 1995]

The affiliation between CAMPlab and CIDCA further reaffirms the association between CAMPlab and autonomy, since CIDCA supplied much of the intellectual backbone of the law. Many of CIDCA's employees remain as outspoken proponents of autonomy, and it remains central to the institution's mission. At times, this association opened doors and allowed CAMPlab staff and participants access to political leaders.

For example, Faran Dometz, a popular coast leader and proponent of autonomy, showed active interest in CAMPlab and organized meetings between CAMPlab staff and participants and regional councilors. Although this association may lend CAMPlab support from advocates of autonomy, the current political climate of Nicaragua is dominated by forces hostile to autonomy. Therefore, the association between CAMPlab and autonomy likely damaged the ability of CAMPlab to secure central government endorsement.

## Shared concerns, common action

Over time, a pattern of shared concerns among CAMPlab participants began to emerge. Three were overarching: general concern for the well-being of their communities, concern for the ability of the area's resource base to sustain their communities, and concern for the maintenance of the rights of their communities.

As a result, a collective identity coalesced based on the identification of common problems that people felt needed to be addressed.

> Interviewer: What did we accomplish in the meeting [on 20 May 1993]?
>
> Mary: They themselves realized that they have problems in common that they can solve.

The shared interest in improved resource management in Pearl Lagoon emerged from the PAR process and continued to be refined and strengthened as insights grew. The collective identity was not only based on rational decisions, but also on emotional inclinations.

> David Howard: This is a feelings thing. You got to have the feelings for protecting natural resources. [September 1995]
>
> Mary: From all the meetings we start having down here, people start getting more interested in the natural resources. Even though some people sense it then it's different if you *feeling*, and I am *feeling*. And when you have a chance to express it.... I think that some people get more conscious about this. So that when these things come up, you could be prepared to know what to say and what you really feel about it. [21 April 1994]

This passion helped the group overcome considerable barriers and gave them confidence that although their numbers were small they were contributing something worthwhile to their community.

> Interviewer: This is hard since people won't have interest until they see results, but CAMP needs the people themselves to make the change.
>
> Johnny: But one person can change the world. And this is a time when people are just getting aware of what are natural resources. Students are thinking about natural resources. Nothing wrong with a small group of people changing things in Pearl Lagoon. [4 July 1994]

Their confidence grew with external validation. For example, when foreign visitors expressed interest in the group's reforestation project, it generated pride among its youth leaders.

> Chris White: This shows us that this was something attractive to other people all over the world. That this is a young group of people working towards something. [13 March 1997]

The group eventually took on a notably social character. A number of times the community group celebrated holidays and members' birthdays together, occasionally at Fine Pine Wood, the park-like stand of mature pine trees near Haulover. The selection of this area seemed natural as it was where church congregations celebrate picnics during the Easter season and where the CAMPlab community group had been actively monitoring and planting trees. These activities solidified friendships and began the process of creating a symbolic space that was associated with the process, further fostering feelings of stewardship of the participants' surroundings.

> Interviewer: Like the social activity, how did you feel about it?

> Mary Bryton: Well, I really feel like it was constructive. It was something good. Because (in the) first place, the people who was there they really get to know how CAMP started, because we have like a historic review... Had some games together... The social activity had an impact on the community and on we ourself, because after we did that, Fine Pine Wood really feel like it was ours. It make it feel like really you was doing something. This is prohibited, this is prohibited to touch. Even if those people don't respect it; those people aren't going to learn from the night to the day. You have to try to stimulate these people. [11 July 1995]

## Discord

Although the process resonated strongly with some community members, these people remained in the minority within the community. To some extent, this was due to a discordance between CAMPlab's objectives or research tools and certain ingrained social norms in Pearl Lagoon. Although the specific suite of social barriers to resource management in Pearl Lagoon is unique, the types of barriers are likely to be shared in other contexts.

These specific barriers are best understood if one considers the history of the coast as a place with a relative abundance of natural resources, but where people are generally marginalized and poor. For most people in Pearl Lagoon, the primary focus is on meeting the immediate needs of the day, not the long-term, seemingly abstract need to manage resources. People may also feel threatened if they believe that resource management will prevent them from fulfilling important social obligations. For example, as Jimmy Bryant said, "It could be an insult to a man to tell a hunter not to hunt. If you tell a hunter not to hunt, he is going to say that he has six children" (19 May 1994).

The congruence between the tenets of resource management and those associated with larger, influential institutions also affected people's acceptance. In Pearl Lagoon, certain religious teachings may reinforce the opinion that management of natural resources is either unnecessary or hubris, especially those that emphasize the impending arrival of the end of the world (Nickerson 1995).

Jimmy Bryant (addressing Kakabila community members): You might say that the end soon come. So we don't think it's important. But let's protect it to the end. [10 May 1994]

Oswaldo Morales, CAMPlab staff member: As I mentioned, I think it is important to talk about culture. Can see culture as very positive and many times as negative.... When talk about the natural resources, [people believe] those thing can't finish. It not important to talk about protecting, because man cannot done [finish] them.... They are there and will be there forever. Things like this.... This is a cultural thing, because [people] see it a different way: man can't affect God's creation. This has to do with education. [6 February 1997]

As a result, CAMPlab staff were necessarily cautious when discussing resource management with some local residents. A clear understanding of their neighbours' social norms placed them at a distinct advantage to an outsider in this regard.

That severe resource depletion is not yet a serious problem on the coast also seemed to make people disinclined to worry about the issues that CAMPlab raised. Memories of astonishing abundance remain strong, particularly among older adults. A young participant commented on the receptivity of adults to his growing concern about the environment.

Gerry: Like they not interested. Don't feel like the natural resources can done [used up] and things like that.

Interviewer: That's interesting, so then they feel like these natural resources, they can't finish?

Gerry Baker: [They say] you can't done this thing then, you know. So it no use in try protecting this thing when you can't done it. Some say, we just hearing about this thing. From so much years we living like the older ones then. So much years we living and this thing never yet done. And we living so long and we have this thing in abundance. [30 June 1994]

However, in some cases, especially among youth living in towns, it is their lack of experience with an environment outside their immediate surroundings that may limit their interest. For example, many of the youth that were taken on forest-monitoring field trips had never seen an intact forest before, even though their small communities are literally surrounded by them.

Gerry Baker: People... they mightn't see a forest. When you don't see something, and you never yet think about this thing in your life, you know, them no pay it no mind neither then. [30 June 1994]

## Other limiting factors

Particular characteristics of the process were challenging for some local people. For example, their desire for immediate, tangible benefits was incongruous with a slow process of change taking place in incremental steps. CAMPlab may have lost the interest of some people because it did not result in immediate benefits.

> Gerry Baker: Round here, I tell you the truth, people don't like [to] attend meeting. I know that. People like go to meeting, if they see action out the meeting.... They don't like have meeting and doing this thing in a future way. For the future, you know. They don't understand that. [30 June 1994]

Intra- and inter-communal divisions also hampered certain efforts, as action research depends on a spirit of cooperation. Religious divisions could be problematic if they raised suspicion of other people. Religious groups do not always teach tolerance of other belief systems. For example, in Pearl Lagoon, there were considerable tensions between the Moravian and the Seventh Day Adventist churches. Each tended to characterize the other's doctrine as misguided.

> Haulover community member: I think that the Adventists are trying to dominate the community. You know there is a lot of tension between the Adventist and Moravian pastors over this. [28 March 1997]

In Haulover, some of the most active participants in CAMPlab were Adventist. Although it has never been explicitly mentioned, and a concerted effort was made to encourage participation from all religious denominations, the potential existed for CAMPlab to be perceived by some as an Adventist-dominated activity.

The ethnic divisions within Pearl Lagoon could also make inter-communal cooperation difficult. The ethnic hierarchy that Hale and Gordon (1987) discussed continues to exist in Pearl Lagoon. In most cases, Pearl Lagoon town residents occupy the position of highest status due to their relative affluence, superior education, and ethnicity (Creole). When Haulover and Pearl Lagoon town members originally met together for CAMPlab meetings, some members felt that this was among the project's most important accomplishments, especially considering that these communities had been on opposing sides of the recent war. Indeed, it represented a remarkable sign of trust when one of CAMPlab's most active members, who had nearly been assassinated during the war by Haulover Contra soldiers, attended meetings in Haulover. Convenience and status issues eventually contributed to the division of this group into two smaller ones.

> Interviewer: What would be the advantage of having it this way instead of having the two communities meet together?

Johnny: Okay, the advantage we will have there is, number one, the people will have more confidence with one another here in Haulover to talk together. You notice in the community you have what you call the fear of talking. A fear of language. A fear of expression. So when ever they would come from Kakabila or these communities, the person will not talk. Because they feel like the people in Pearl Lagoon town are more advance. So they feel that this person would laugh at them. [22 June 1995]

Social norms also shaped the actions that people chose to take. For example, the youthfulness of CAMPlab's Haulover communal group was one factor that defined the range of options for action. Youth are rarely civil activists or political leaders in coast communities due to social norms that encourage people to look to male adults for political leadership. So although youth may feel that environmental issues are best appreciated by their generation, they may not feel empowered to take action beyond the traditional social roles available to them.

Interviewer: What do you feel could be done about these problems? Any ideas?

Steve Jason: I think the only thing really is to talk... that's all. Could talk to the people. Because sometime you talk and it rare people listen to you, but at least you trying to warn them.

Felix Hing: I feel that idea would be for our generation, because many of our parent lacking more onto this. [student group interview, 19 October 1994]

Some planned activities, even though developed by the communal groups themselves, were not implemented because they would require a level of confidence that was unusual for any communal member, especially for youth. For example, young women did not feel comfortable going house-to-house to talk about resource issues with their neighbours. Ageism has had a particular impact on the participation of CAMPlab Haulover group in the process of developing a management plan. Although youth may have been encouraged to be involved in *de facto* management, such as reforestation, the opportunities for them to participate with adult leaders in a policy-establishing process remained limited.

## Conclusions

As CAMPlab passed through various periods of activity and quiescence, individuals such as Mary, Jessica, Edwin, Johnny, and Chris came forward to lead and sustain the process. They volunteered considerable time and effort and demonstrated considerable perseverance. These participants were, in large part, motivated to support CAMPlab to the extent that the project resonated with their values and aspirations. In particular, CAMPlab resonated with some people's desire for a strong resource base and communal rights that CAMPlab shared with the autonomy movement. Their experiences, shared values, and social bonds have served as the base for a collective identity associated with CAMPlab.

An understanding of the embeddedness of CAMPlab in this particular social context helps explain the viability of the process at the level of Pearl Lagoon. The substantive message of CAMPlab clearly resonated with a group of Pearl Lagoon residents, but the unique socioeconomic conditions and social norms of the context have limited the number of people who share this orientation. The process itself was either engaging or uninspiring depending on one's interests in natural resource management and tolerance for a slow, group-oriented process. However, for a growing number of people, the process resonated with their aspirations for a future defined by well-being, a strong natural resource base, and secure community rights.

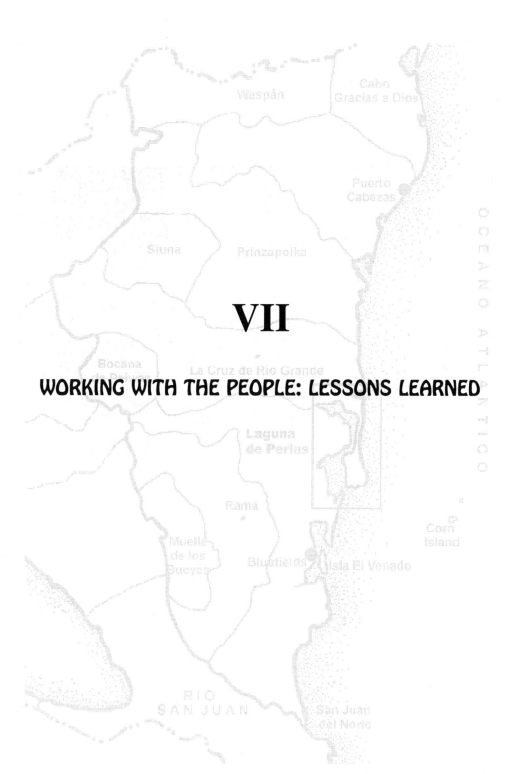

# VII

## WORKING WITH THE PEOPLE: LESSONS LEARNED

Photo: Patrick Christie

# 7. WORKING WITH THE PEOPLE: LESSONS LEARNED

*David Bradford, Ronnie Vernooy, Patrick Christie, Ray Garth,
Bonifacio González, Mark Hostetler, Oswaldo Morales,
Bertha Simmons, Eduardo Tinkam, Noreen White*

Mary: I see CAMP born and grow. I would like to see CAMP to reach to be something big then. Become one of the movement that help to take care of the natural resources that we have. Something coming from people, not from a political work. [11 July 1995]

The CAMPlab experience taught us many lessons. The project not only increased the body of evidence in favour of participatory action research (PAR), but it also contributed to the development of practical mechanisms for empowering indigenous and ethnic communities and engaging them, together with institutions and local governments, in making decisions that affect their environment and livelihoods. In addition, the CAMPlab experience resulted in concrete steps toward the conservation and management of the natural resource base that supports the Pearl Lagoon communities, most notably in the form of the management plan.

In this chapter we discuss the lessons learned during the project, focusing on the process of participation, the results, and the impact. In terms of assessing process and methods, first, we look at whether and how CAMPlab has achieved the two main goals and four core features of a PAR approach (see chapter 1). Second, we discuss the factors that influence the practice of PAR either positively or negatively. Third, we summarize CAMPlab's contribution to a new way of problem-solving and policymaking on Nicaragua's Caribbean coast.

### Achieving PAR goals: moving toward critical consciousness

> Bluefields resident: One thing that impress me about CAMPlab is how the project encourage the people to test their own water and after finding out by their own practice that some of the wells have high concentration of coliforms, the people themselves decided, without any saying or doing from the Ministry of Health, to condemn one well and to put chlorine in the other wells to make the water good for drinking. [November 1999]

PAR is different from other forms of research in its emphasis on social change and empowerment of people. These two goals are functionally integrated, as empowerment is the principal engine driving social change. The focus is usually on developing a critical consciousness of oppressive social relationships that can be used to catalyze and sustain activism. Increasingly, and in the case of CAMPlab, attention has been on supplementing information about social relationships with knowledge about the biophysical world that supports communities. In discussing whether CAMPlab has made strides toward attaining the principal goals of PAR, it is necessary to assess whether critical consciousness was raised and whether this motivated people to act.

Four key features set the PAR process in motion. Practitioners have abandoned the supposed objective, reductionist paradigm of most social science in favour of one that explicitly embraces the need for research methods that directly address oppressive relationships. As a first step, the reorganization of the traditional subject–object research relationship into a co-learning interaction that fosters a subject–subject relationship is fundamental. The focus on a transformative research process that demands attention to process as well as output is a distinguishing feature. Finally, the explicit, simultaneous linking of reflection and action as natural, mutually supporting processes is an important mechanism by which the critical consciousness of participants is raised.

For the past 6 years, CAMPlab has consistently been guided by these four features. It has attempted to address the relationships that have marginalized Pearl Lagoon communities from the decision-making processes that determine how local natural resources are used. This has required that local community members assemble a body of knowledge and experience that they can draw on when they engage in a dialogue with others. The creation of this knowledge base represents the unification of new exogenous and local knowledge.

Knowledge about the area's natural resources, which existed in a diffuse manner throughout the communities, is being gathered, assessed, and disseminated in a regular and coherent way. CAMPlab staff, made up of Costeños assisted by occasional external advisors, has entered into a partnership with local residents in such endeavours. On occasion, it was tempting to rely on traditional, nonparticipatory

148

research methods and to act on behalf of communities to expedite an outcome, but generally, staff have maintained an interactive, balanced relationship with the project's constituency. Maintaining a balanced relationship has required a considerable degree of self-awareness on the part of the staff. Time for dialogue among staff, through training or evaluations, has been necessary for creating conscientious staff members. This has resulted in the outpouring of considerable support for the program from communities and a feeling of local ownership of CAMPlab. Men and women, and in particular youth, have joined the movement that is seen as belonging to the local people, not to a political party.

The engagement of staff and community participants in both information collection and action has a number of implications. First, the interest level of local residents increases if action is an explicit part of the research process. (Research for research's sake is of little interest to most local people.) For example, tree planting was consistently of interest to local people. Afterwards, participants would visit and monitor planted areas without needing notice or reminders from project staff.

Second, the lessons drawn from action experiences are cycled into and become part of the collective psyche of those involved. These lessons then inform future actions; for example, initial failures of reforestation due to location and timing led to more successful subsequent attempts.

## Strides forward

Conflicts are the midwives of consciousness. [Horton and Freire 1990, p. 187]

As documented in chapters 5 and 6, CAMPlab engaged the residents of Pearl Lagoon in a process of discovery. By their own account, many residents learned for the first time how to assess and manage their natural resources in a systematic manner. Their interest in these matters is grounded in a deeply held belief that these natural resources are the sustenance of their communities. Local communities have struggled for control over these resources for generations, most recently by supporting the autonomy process.

In a sense, CAMPlab has become a local manifestation of autonomy. It has allowed individuals and groups of individuals to become directly involved in matters that profoundly affect their lives. It has also served as a vehicle by which communities can engage in a meaningful dialogue with their government. Considering the historic boundaries between the state and these communities, such a transformation does not take place without a certain degree of struggle.

The communities of Pearl Lagoon have become motivated to engage the government in a dialogue concerning the management of their natural resources. For example, the historic, assumed right of Pearl Lagoon's mayor to give permission unilaterally to loggers to harvest communal forests has been challenged. This year, when the Haulover community prevented the logging of Pinal, after the mayor had given a logger permission to remove trees without community consultation, the relationship between community and its elected leaders changed in a fundamental way.

Similarly, CAMPlab's mobilization of communities to become involved in a critical evaluation of the DIPAL management plan for the area's fisheries resources created a new dimension in the relation between central government agencies and communities. These are small, but significant steps toward active participation of communities in the management of their affairs. Increasingly, government agencies are learning that their actions are not only being observed, as has always been the case, but that they are increasingly accountable to their constituents.

Furthermore, CAMPlab has helped raise the bar for other projects in the area. By involving community members in substantive project decisions (e.g., planning, funding decisions, staff selection, etc.), the project has shown that community members cannot be treated as mere beneficiaries of programs; rather, they are collaborators in determining the direction of programs that affect their communities.

CAMPlab has also profoundly affected the project's implementing agency, CIDCA. In the early 1990s this institution was a hierarchical organization employing mainly traditional research methods. After considerable struggle between CAMPlab staff and CIDCA administrators, institutional structures that were more conducive to PAR (i.e., horizontal and decentralized) were established. The fact that CIDCA has now embraced PAR and uses its work in Pearl Lagoon as an example, especially in terms of forest resource management and land tenure, is an important institutional shift that brings CIDCA and the communities together in a more unified front. CAMPlab has given the institution a new identity in terms of its role as a research centre, providing a critical link between research and development in one of the poorest and most isolated regions of the Americas.

CIDCA, whose mission is to strengthen the autonomy process through research and studies that contribute to the solution of specific problems, has identified land tenure issues and natural resource management as critical to the consolidation of the autonomy process. Both are intrinsically related as community resource management and planning serve as spatial justification for the territorial claims of indigenous peoples. According to the views of CIDCA, territorial claims will not only be based on the historical use of land and water resources, but also on the plans that communities have for the future management of their resources. The experience in the Pearl Lagoon is a case study in how to put this insight into practice.

That meaningful change is slow and painful is predictable and well documented. Conflict truly has been the midwife of change for Pearl Lagoon. There have been conflicts with CIDCA over project management and conflicts with government agencies over the right of communities to take part in the development of resource management plans. That elites have referred to the CAMPlab process as subversive indicates at least modest success. The labeling of this process as such is an attempt to disqualify those who are attempting to change longstanding, unequal relations. It also indicates to elites that the status quo is being questioned.

## Enabling and constraining factors

Based on our experience to date, the goals and methods of the CAMPlab project and the researchers' actions were perceived by many local people to be close to their interests and experiences. Resonance in these three key areas explains the considerable involvement in the PAR process and the feedback into it.

This resonance is reflected in both the quality of the management plan and the broad endorsement of the plan. It is also reflected in the various manifestations of the organizational capacity or potential of the people. When their livelihoods seemed to be threatened, this potential took the form of collective action. For example, they put pressure on large-scale fishers from Bluefields who they thought were overfishing, and also on the fish plant to prevent the distribution of fine-mesh gill nets, which they thought were killing too many juvenile fish.

The possibility of collective responses such as these was enhanced by three factors:

- Common interest, in terms of the shared experience of these people, who depend on the local environment and especially the lagoon for subsistence, increases the potential for collective responses in many instances.

- The feeling of community ownership of local resources is strengthened by both communal titles to land and the Autonomy Law, which are seen by many as platforms for asserting local ownership and the right to control their territories and the natural resources within them.

- CAMPlab played an important role in increasing the communities' organizational capacity and knowledge base.

It is worth keeping in mind that the project started from nothing in terms of local PAR capabilities, although, as the results obtained so far demonstrate, there clearly was latent potential. The most important element related to this factor has been the deployment of communal investigators motivated by and interested in the central research questions. Even though they had different backgrounds, expertise, and experience, the core team of communal investigators and their counterparts in the communities together in the CAMPlab committees have been instrumental in providing a strong local base for the research process.

Initially, the project focused on a few communities, but because of the nature of the resource base, was expanded to cover the whole basin. One of the project's goals was to involve individuals from diverse backgrounds. Therefore, men and women, community leaders, municipal authorities, and regional government officials were encouraged to participate in CAMPlab. Special attention was paid to getting young people involved.

In terms of social structure, the goals set by the project might be considered very ambitious. As discussed in chapters 2, 3 and 4, Pearl Lagoon basin is characterized by a highly diverse and complex ecology, a multi-ethnic population (with a variety of languages and religions), and a complex and ever-changing set of survival and livelihood strategies, combining fishing, agriculture, hunting and collecting, petty trade, and income from foreign sources. These many variables create a complex image. Tentatively, one might conclude that the ambitious nature of the participatory process and the significant geographic scope, combined with this diversity, have had an important constraining effect, particularly in terms of participation. In addition, there still exist certain imbalances in terms of gender: men tend to occupy most of the leadership roles and predominate in decision-making.

Chapters 5 and 6 show that the process of communal empowerment leading to social change requires great patience. At times, staff and community members naturally became frustrated with the slow pace of change. The level of complexity of the issues, that have at times overwhelmed a still relatively small group of staff and committed community members, should not be underestimated. PAR processes are usually time and resources intensive, and the CAMPlab experience is no exception. A great deal of time is required to build and train a core team and to establish and train local cohorts of the team in the communities. Designing, conducting, and monitoring research has also been very time intensive.

External funding, although relatively modest, was necessary to hire and retain core staff and to cover such research expenses as transportation (which is difficult in this region), meetings, and training events, and the equipment for resource monitoring. Thus far, the CAMPlab process has been able to obtain the financial assistance of institutions that value its continuation. Although we believe that these funds have been put to wise use, the dependence of such processes on external human and financial support is worrisome. In the long term, such support should come from local and sustainable sources. For a program that is not in line with the current Nicaraguan government's neoliberal development agenda, the struggle to survive financially will be a continuous one. Undoubtedly, it is prudent to investigate means of internal financial support and ways to reduce project expenses.

Training has played an important role in strengthening the capacities of the core research team and the community members. Weaknesses remain, however, and with the move toward implementation of the management plan, new research skills and tools may need to be added to the project's portfolio, such as policy analysis and review, legal knowledge (e.g., related to decentralization), and enhanced participatory monitoring and evaluation skills. Skills to conduct gender analysis and process documentation could be further strengthened.

Factors more external to the project have also influenced its evolution. The communities' reactions to changes caused by greater commercialization of the fisheries indicate that local people want to protect their resources through better management and control of exploitation. As we saw in chapter 4, most of the men and women interviewed were concerned about the future of the fisheries and, therefore, the future of their communities. Many suggested that some form of regulations should be imposed. However, people also pointed to the difficulty of limiting fishing when there are so few other economic alternatives. The future of agriculture, for example, depends on a stable market — not easily achieved on the Atlantic coast or in the country as a whole.

People of Pearl Lagoon are generally concerned about people from outside using and, more important, abusing the lagoon's resources. However, they are not strongly opposed to allowing outsiders to fish in the lagoon provided that everyone uses the methods employed by the community, which tend to be small scale. There is an unwillingness to deny anyone the ability to feed themselves, but there are concerns that outsiders should not overtax the lagoon's resources.

Conversely, the central government's lack of respect for and enforcement of the Autonomy Law and land titles, as well as its lack of support for the regional autonomous governments in the RAAS and RAAN, has had a negative effect on the organizational capacity of the communities. Engagement with elites and the defenders of the status quo is the nature of PAR. Thus far, participants in the CAMPlab process have learned much from initial interactions with those with vested interests. Early, "naive" interactions with government agencies illustrated that co-opting of the process to serve vested interests is a likely outcome unless vigilance is maintained. The fact that CAMPlab is now, again, being approached by these agencies to collaborate represents both an opportunity and a challenge.

In terms of the global economy, it might be argued that the involvement of Pearl Lagoon in international markets is not new, even though today's demands are higher then ever before and resources are fewer. CAMPlab has showed that the communities have mixed feelings about these new market opportunities. This should serve as a warning signal for the local proponents of development through "competitive advantage" or increasing specialization of the systems of production. Chapter 4 gives us insight into the changes in production patterns and people's opinions about the growing tendency of communities to specialize in fishing. The Pearl Lagoon experience also shows that people have ideas for dealing with the threat of being caught up in a single form of production that would make their communities more vulnerable in the long run. They are looking for opportunities to market their agricultural products. Based on this, markets that mimic the historical cycles of production and the close connectedness of the systems of production (fishing, agriculture, forest use, hunting) in the basin, might be more stable and sustainable in the long run than the new trend toward specialization.

## Changing the institutional approach

Perhaps the most important result of the project so far has been its influence on the institutional approach to solving problems related to management of natural resources. This contribution encompasses several elements. One is the willingness of the RAAS's council to create a legal precedent by passing a resolution (regional law) concerning the management plan. This occurred after some counselors had personally verified that CAMPlab has been a fully horizontal process with the strong participation of the community leaders of the Pearl Lagoon basin. This was also acknowledged by the central government representatives, who are trying to develop the fisheries sector in the area, in particular through the DIPAL project. CAMPlab's reputation is no doubt strengthening the legitimacy of the PAR process to address issues concerning resource management. It also reinforces local people's positions, views and efforts concerning the management of natural resources of the basin and their success in finally "being heard" by the government after all these years.

The same could be said about decision-making at the municipal level. The municipal council of Pearl Lagoon and the mayor are clearly interested in making the management plan a municipal ordinance. This move is of critical importance, because, as Reilly (1997) has pointed out, mayors, unlike other members of the political class, have to deal with the everyday problems brought to them as there is no place to hide from their constituents "in rhetorical flourishes or grand statements of policy," which is what central and regional government officials usually do during their visits to the area.

However, there are some problems yet to be solved at this level — among them is the forthcoming municipal election, which may delay the official declaration and approval of the management plan as the new mayor may not be familiar with the process. A second problem may be the lack of capacity to enforce the standards set by the ordinance, given that Pearl Lagoon is a relatively new municipality. Nevertheless, we think that the municipality represents the best option for the implementation of a successful comanagement strategy. The challenge will be to be creative and strong enough to fill in the spaces that the decentralization process and the state reform currently being proposed in Nicaragua are likely to produce.

**154**

# A continuing struggle

Political parties come and go, people remain and their problems constantly deserve attention and support. Vested interests are everywhere so that an important part of participatory research work is to face up to them and try to succeed. Our work is rather cyclical and it depends on constancy. Thus if you can sustain your work at the lagoon, I believe it would still be useful. [Orlando Fals-Borda, quoted in Christie 1999, pp. 458–459]

CAMPlab served as a catalyst to mobilize the marginalized coastal communities facing or foreseeing a serious conflict over access to natural resources. In Pearl Lagoon, control of the resources is contested by various actors including private interests, the government, indigenous communities, and, indirectly, Mestizo farmers.

CAMPlab has shown that when the relationship between the communities and the state — represented at the national level by DIPAL, MARENA, and the Instituto Nicaragüense de Reforma Agraria (INRA), at the regional level by the autonomous government, and at the local level by the municipal government — is poor due to the government's failure to define indigenous rights, there is a tendency toward confrontation. As a result, comanagement initiatives tend to fail.

CAMPlab has also shown that local communities feel that the government should pay more attention to their problems. They demand the right to participate in the planning and formulation of solutions for these problems. A path toward comanagement is being built in the Pearl Lagoon basin, although slowly, based on direct communication between the two major stakeholders: the communities and the government institutions.

The peoples of the Caribbean coast of Nicaragua have a long history of struggle for recognition and self-determination, the spirit of which is captured in the Autonomy Law. As we have argued, CAMPlab conforms to people's historical aspirations by fostering community solidarity, organization, and leadership. It builds on previous demands and supports people's ideas for innovative forms of collective management, a goal that is receiving increasing support at various levels.

A number of shortcoming must still be overcome, however. The quantity and quality of participation could be improved by further strengthening the research capabilities and facilitation skills of core CAMPlab staff and CAMPlab committees in the communities. Among other benefits, this would allow them to reach out to a larger group of people, involving young people more actively, and balancing

**155**

the current unequal participation of men and women, in terms of numbers and kinds of involvement in the process. Training in participatory monitoring and evaluation techniques would provide a stronger base for reflection about these and other issues pertaining to participation, including an analysis of the meaning of "community" and the gendered nature of decision-making processes. Construction of the road toward autonomy has advanced, but it is not yet complete.

Photo: CIDCA

# BIBLIOGRAPHY

Barbee, S. 1997. Women as agriculture producers in the Pearl Lagoon. Wani, 22, 6-22.

Barrett, B. 1994a. Salud y cultura en la RAAS. Wani, 15, 20-37.
_____ 1994b. Medicinal plants of Nicaragua's Atlantic coast. Economic Botany, 48(1), 8-20.

Bentley, J.W. 1994. Facts, fantasies, and failures of farmer participatory research. Agriculture and Human Values, Spring-Summer, 140-150.

Bernacsek, G.M. 1984. Approaches to analyzing the relationship between catch and effort in tropical artisanal fisheries using the example of Tanzania. *In* Kapetsky, J.M.; Lasserre, G. ed. Management of coastal lagoon fisheries. Food and Agriculture Organisation, Rome, Italy. Studies and reviews GFCM 61(1). pp. 198-231.

Bouwsma, H.; Sánchez, R.; van der Hoeven, J.J.; Rosales, D. 1997. Plan de manejo integral para los recursos hidrobiológicos de la Cuenca de Laguna de Perlas y la desembocadura del Río Grande. Proyecto para el Desarrollo Integral de la Pesca Artesanal en Laguna de Perlas (DIPAL) and Centro de Investigación de los Recursos Hidrobiológicos (CIRH), Pearl Lagoon, Nicaragua.

Butler, J. 1997. The peoples of the Atlantic Coast. *In* Walker, T.W. ed., Nicaragua without illusions: regime transition and structural adjustment in the 1990s. Scholarly Resources Inc., Wilmington, DE, USA. pp. 219-234.

CACRC (Central American and Caribbean Research Council). 1996. Diagnóstico general sobre la tenencia de la tierra en las comunidades indígenas de Nicaragua. Department of Anthropology, University of Texas, Austin, TX, USA. Project description.
_____ 1998. Diagnóstico general sobre la tenencia de la tierra en las comunidades indígenas de la costa Atlántica. III Vol. (Marco General, Resumen Ejecutivo, Informe final). Department of Anthropology, University of Texas, Austin, TX, USA. Consultoría 084-96.

Caddy, J.F. 1989. Marine invertebrate fisheries: their assessment and management. John Wiley and Sons, New York, NY, USA.

Carr, A.F. 1992. High jungles and low (2nd ed.). University Press of Florida, Gainesville, FL, USA.

Cattle, D.J. 1976. Dietary diversity and nutritional security in a coastal Miskito indian village, eastern Nicaragua. *In* Helms, M.W.; Loveland, F.O., ed., Frontier adaptations in lower Central America. Institute for the Study of Human Issues, Philadelphia, PA, USA. pp. 117-130.

Christie, P. 1993. The development and evaluation of participatory integrated coastal assessment as used in Pearl Lagoon, the Southern Atlantic Coast of Nicaragua. University of Michigan, Ann Arbor, MI, USA. Master's thesis.

_____ 1999. "In a country without forest, no life is good:" participatory action research in the neo-liberal context of Nicaragua. University of Michigan, MI, USA. PhD dissertation.

Cicin-Sain, B.; Knecht, R.W. 1998. Integrated coastal and ocean management: concepts and practices. Island Press, Washington, DC, USA.

CIDCA (Centro de Investigaciones y Documentación de la Costa Atlántica). 1987. Ethnic groups and the nation state: the case of the Atlantic Coast in Nicaragua. Department of Social Anthropology, University of Stockholm, Stockholm, Sweden.

_____ 1989. Estudio de la Región Autonóma del Atlántico Sur. CIDCA, Bluefields, Nicaragua.

CIDCA-CAMPlab (in cooperation with the communities of Pearl Lagoon). 1999. Plan de manejo integral normativo de los recursos naturales del municipio de Pearl Lagoon, RAAS (borrador). Universidad Centroamericana/Centro de Investigaciones y Documentación de la Costa Atlántica CAMPlab, Haulover, Nicaragua.

CIDCA-UCA (Centro de Investigaciones y Documentación de la Costa Atlántica and Universidad CentroAmericana). 1996. Diagnóstico de las regiones autonómas y elementos para el plan de acción de CIDCA en el periódo 1997-2002. CIDCA, Bilwi, Nicaragua. Internal document.

Clewell, A.F. 1986. Observations on the vegetation of the Mosquitia in Honduras. SIDA, 11(3), 258-270.

Cominsky, S. 1976. Carib-Creole relations in a Belizean community. *In* Helms, M.W.; Loveland, F.O., ed., Frontier adaptations in lower Central America. Institute for the Study of Human Issues, Philadelphia, PA, USA. pp. 95-114.

Connell, J.H. 1978. Diversity in tropical rain forests and coral reefs. Science, 199, 1302-1310.

Corrales, D.; Shión, M.; Tuomasjukka, T. 1996. Diagnóstico forestal de Nicaragua. Study conducted for the International Union for the Conservation of Nature (IUCN), Managua, Nicaragua. Draft.

Cyens, R. 1992. Nicaragua's Miskito Coast braces for a resource war. The Wall Street Journal, September 4, A9.

Davidson, W.V. 1976. Black Carib (Garifuna) habitats in Central America. *In* Helms, M.W.; Loveland, F.O. ed., Frontier adaptations in lower Central America. Institute for the study of Human Issues, Philadelphia, PA, USA. pp. 85-94.

Day, J.W.; Hall, C.A.; Kemp, W.M.; Yañez-Arancibia, A. 1989. Estuarine ecology. John Wiley and Sons, New York, NY, USA.

DIPAL (Desarrollo Integral de la Pesca Artesanal en Laguna de Perlas) 1996a. Informe preliminar sobre los resultados de las investigaciones hidrológicas realizadas en la Cuenca de Lagunas de Perlas. Pearl Lagoon, Nicaragua. Project report.
_____ 1996b. Informe preliminar sobre los resultados de las investigaciones pesqueras realizadas en la Cuenca de Laguna de Perlas. Pearl Lagoon, Nicaragua. Project report.
_____ 1999. Informe. Pearl Lagoon, Nicaragua. Project report.
Dozier, C.L. 1985. Nicaragua's Mosquito Shore, the years of British and American presence. University of Alabama Press, Tuscaloosa, AL, USA.

ECLAC (Economic Commission for Latin America and the Caribbean). 1996. Statistical Yearbook for Latin America and the Caribbean. United Nations, Santiago, Chile.
_____ 1997. Statistical Yearbook for Latin America and the Caribbean. United Nations, Santiago, Chile.

Ehrhardt, N.M.; Perez, M.;Sánchez, R. 1995. Dinámica de producción de los recursos camaroneros de Nicaragua. Centro de Investigación de Recursos Hidrobiológicos (CIRH) and Ministerio de Economía y Desarrollo (MEDE), Managua, Nicaragua.

Ehrhardt, N.M.; Sánchez, R. 1995. Evaluación de la pesquería de camarón rojo *Peaeus duorarum* y *Penaeus brasiliensis* en la Costa Caribe de Nicaragua. Centro de Investigación de Recursos Hidrobiológicos, Managua, Nicaragua.

Elizondo, D. 1997. The environment. *In* Nicaragua without illusions: regime transition and structural adjustment in the 1990s. Scholarly Resources Inc., Wilmington, DE, USA. pp. 131-145.

Fals-Borda, O.; Rahman, R.A. 1991. Action and knowledge: breaking the monopoly with participatory action-research. Apex Press, New York, NY, USA.

FAO (Food and Agricultural Organisation). 1997. State of the world's forests. FAO, Rome, Italy.
_____ 1998. Statistical databases. http://apps.fao.org/

Ferrer, E.M.; Polotan de la Cruz, L.; Domingo, M.A. ed. 1996. Seeds of hope. College of Social Work and Community Development, University of the Philippines, Manila, Philippines.

Found, W.C. 1995. Participatory research and development: an assessment of IDRC's experience and prospects. International Development Research Centre, Ottawa, ON, Canada.

Freire, P. 1992. Education for critical consciousness (2nd ed.). Continuum, New York, NY, USA.

Freire, P. 1993. Pedagogy of the oppressed (2nd ed.). Continuum. New York, NY, USA.

García, N.H.; Camacho, J.J. 1994. Informe sobre manglares de Nicaragua. *In* Suman, D., ed., El Ecosistema de manglar en América Latina y la Cuenca del Caribe: su manejo y conservación. Rosentiel School of Marine and Atmospheric Science, University of Miami, Miami, FL, USA. pp. 160-167.

Gordon, E.T. 1991. La mujer costeña en la pesca artesanal. Wani, 9, 66-73.
_____ 1998. Disparate diaspora. Indentity and politics in an African-Nicaraguan community. University of Texas Press, Austin, TX, USA.

Greaves, A. 1978. Description of seed sources and collections for provenances of *Pinus caribaea*. Unit of Tropical Silviculture, Commonwealth Forestry Institute, University of Oxford, UK.

Guilfoyle, K.J. 1994. A case study of the effects of human exploitation and hurricane damage upon the mangrove ecosystems of Laguna Perlas, Nicaragua. Hampshire College, Amherst, MA, USA. BS thesis.

Hale, C.R.; Gordon, E.T. 1987. Historical and contemporary demography of Nicaragua's Atlantic coast. *In* Ethnic groups and the nation state: the case of the Atlantic coast in Nicaragua. University of Stockholm, Stockholm, Sweden. pp. 6-31.

Helms, M. 1969. Asang: adaptations to cultural contact in a Miskito community. University of Florida Press, Gainsville, FL, USA.
_____ 1971. Purchase society: adaptation to economic frontiers. Anthropological Quarterly, 42(4), 325-342.

Hilborn, R.; Walters, C.J. 1992. Quantitative fisheries stock assessment: choice, dynamics and uncertainty. Chapman and Hall, New York. NY, USA.

Hinchcliffe, F.; Thompson, J.; Pretty, J.; Guijt, I.; Shah, P., ed.1999. Fertile ground. The impacts of participatory watershed management. International Institute for Environment and Development/Intermediate Technology Publications, London, UK.

Holstein, J.A.; Gubrium, J.F. 1995. The active interview. Sage Publications, Thousand Oaks, CA, USA.

Hopkins, J.S.; Sandifer, P.A.; DeVoe, M.R.; Holland, A.F; Browdy, C.L.; Stokes, A.D. 1995. Environmental impacts of shrimp farming with special reference to the situation in the continental United States. Estuaries, 18(1A), 25-42.

Horton, M.; Freire, P. 1990. We make the road by walking: conversations on education and social change. Temple University Press, Philadelphia, PA, USA.

Hostetler, M. 1998. Local reactions to capitalist change in the fisheries of Pearl Lagoon on the Atlantic coast of Nicaragua. Simon Fraser University, Vancouver, BC, Canada. Master's thesis.

Howard, S. 1993. El caso de la RAAN: autonomía y derechos territoriales indígenas. Wani, 14, 1-15.

IDRC (International Development Research Centre). 1988. Participatory research in IDRC. IDRC, Ottawa, ON, Canada. Working group paper.

INDERA (Instituto de Desarrollo para las Regiones Autonómas). 1991. Diagnóstico de los recursos pesqueros, Región Autonóma Atlántico Sur. INDERA, Managua, Nicaragua.

INEC (Instituto Nacional de Estadísticas y Censos). 1996. Resumen censal. VII censo nacional de población y III de vivienda, 1995. INEC, Managua, Nicaragua.

IPADE (Instituto para el Desarrollo de la Democracia). 1995. Listado de propiedades de las comunidades indígenas de las Regiones Autonómas. IPADE, Bluefields, Nicaragua.

IRENA (Instituto de Recursos Naturales y del Medio Ambiente). 1990. Especies para reforestación: pino. IRENA, Managua, Nicaragua. Technical note 6.

Isaac, V.J. 1988. Synopsis of biological data on the whitemouth croaker, *Micropogonias furnieri* (Desmarest, 1823). Food and Agriculture Organisation, Rome Italy. Fisheries synopsis 150.

Jamieson, M.A. 1995. Kinship and gender as political processes among the Miskitu of Eastern Nicaragua. London School of Economics and Political Science, London, UK. PhD dissertation.
_____ 1999. El inglés y la variedad de miskito en la cuenca de Laguna de Perlas. Wani, 24, 22-33.

Kapestky, J.M. 1981. Some considerations for the management of coastal lagoon fisheries. Food and Agriculture Organisation, Rome Italy. Fisheries technical paper 218.

Kapetsky, J.M.; Lasserre, G., ed., 1984. Management of coastal lagoon fisheries: studies and reviews GFCM (61) vol. 1 and 2. Food and Agriculture Organisation, Rome, Italy.

Kasch, K.; Kennedy, M.; Nagel, A.; Colon, M.; Castillo, A.C.; Anderson, R.; Somarriba, S . 1989. Regional study of Pearl Lagoon. Arquitectos y Planificadores de Apoyo a Nicaragua (APSNICA), Bluefields, Nicaragua.

Kjerfve, B.; Magill, K.E.. 1989. Geographic and hydrodynamic characteristics of shallow coastal lagoons. Marine Geology, 88, 187-199.

Lightburn, M.; Sánchez, J.; Sandino de Hernández, S. 1981. Muestreos biológicos de camarones en lagunas marginales de la Costa Atlántica de Nicaragua. Report for the Centro de Investigaciones Pesqueros (CIP-INPESCA), Managua, Nicaragua.

MacDonald, T. 1988. The moral economy of the Miskito indians: local roots of geopolitical conflict. *In* Guidieri, R.; Pellizzi, F.; Tambiah, S.J., ed., Ethnicities and nations: processes of interethnic relations in Latin America, Southeast Asia and the Pacific. Rothko Chapel, Houston, TX, USA, pp. 107-153.

Mallona, M.A. 1992. Impact of hurricane Joan on sapling survival, growth, and recruitment in the southeast coast of Nicaragua. University of Michigan, Ann Arbor, MI, USA. Master's thesis.

Marshall, M.J.; Peralta, L.; Foote, J.L. 1995. Lagoonal reconnaissance and near coastal fish surveys in the Miskito Coast protected area. Mote Marine Laboratory, Sarasota, FL, USA. Report 417.

Martínez, S. 1993. Pesquerías de camarón y langostas en Nicaragua. Centro de Investigación de Recursos Hidrobiológicos (CIRH), Managua, Nicaragua.

McAllister, K. 1999. Understanding participation: monitoring and evaluating process, outputs and outcomes. International Development Research Centre, Ottawa, ON, Canada.

McClusky, D.S. 1981. The estuarine ecosystem. John Wiley and Sons, New York, NY, USA.

McMichael, R.H.; Peters, K.M.; Parsons, G.R. 1989. Early life history of the snook, *Centropomus undecimalis*, in Tampa Bay, Florida. Northeast Gulf Science, 10(2), 113-125.

MEDE-PESCA (Ministerio de Economía y Desarrollo/Desarrollo de la Pesca). 1993. Proyecto piloto para el Desarrollo Integral de Pesca Artesanal en Laguna de Perlas (DIPAL). Ministerio de Economía y Desarrollo, Bluefields, Nicaragua. Project document.

Mitchell, M.K.; Stapp, W.B. 1993. Field manual for water quality monitoring. Thomas Shore, Dexter, MI, USA.

Morenza, M. 1992. Fishing-biological analysis of commercial shrimps at the Bay of Cienfuegos. Revista Cubana de Investigación Pesquera, 16(3-4), 1-12.

Nickerson, V. 1995. Telling stories: community history as a tool for natural resource managers. University of Michigan, Ann Arbor, MI, USA. Master's thesis.

Nietschmann, B. 1972. Hunting and fishing focus among the Miskito indians, eastern Nicaragua. Human Ecology, 1, 41-67.
_____ 1973. Between land and water: the subsistence ecology of the Miskito indians, eastern Nicaragua. Seminar Press, New York, NY, USA.

**162**

Nitlapán 1993. Tendencias actuales de la frontera agrícola en Nicaragua. Universidad CentroAmericana, Managua, Nicaragua. Consultant's report to the Agencia Sueca para el Desarrollo Internacional.

Parsons, J.J. 1955. The Miskito pine savanna of Nicaragua and Honduras. Annals of the Association of American Geographers, 23(4), 15-28.

Peterson, M.S.; Gilmore, R.G. Jr. 1991. Eco-physiology of juvenile snook *Centropomus undecimalis* (Bloch): life-history implications. Bulletin of Marine Sciences, 48(1), 46-57.

Pottier, J. 1995. Ethics, empowerment and the research process. *In* Pottier, J.; Lobo, M., ed., African food systems under stress. Desktop Display, Brighton, UK. pp. 254-267.

Radley, J. 1960. The physical geography of the east coast of Nicaragua. University of California at Berkeley, USA. Master's thesis.

Reilly, C.A. 1997. Mayors, Mayans and poets. Grassroots Development, Journal of the Inter-American Foundation, 21(1), 5-11.

Robins, C.R.; Ray, G.C. 1986. A field guide to Atlantic coast fishes, North America. Houghton Mifflin Co., Boston, USA.

Robinson, S. 1991. Diagnóstico preliminar de la situación actual del medio ambiente en la Region Autonóma Atlántico Sur (RAAS). Instituto de Desarrollo para las Regiones Autonómas, Managua, Nicaragua.

Roth, L.C.; Grijalva, A. 1991. New record of the mangrove, *Pelliciera rhizophorae*, on the Atlantic coast of Nicaragua. Rhodora, 93(874), 183-186.

Roustan, M.C.; Robinson, S. 1997. Informe de evaluación intermedia proyecto CAMP-LAB. Ayuda Popular Noruega (APN), Managua, Nicaragua, and International Development Research Centre (IDRC), Ottawa, Canada. Project evaluation report.

Rutherford, E.S.; Schmidt, T.W.; Tilmant, J.T. 1986. The early life history of spotted seatrout, red drum, gray snapper, and snook in Everglades National Park. National Park Service, Homestead, FL, USA. Report SFRC - 86/07.

Ryan, J. 1990. Water quality survey: Pearl Lagoon and Orinoco. Ayuda Popular Noruega (APN), Managua, Nicaragua. Internal report.
_____ 1992. Medioambientes marinos de la Costa Caribe de Nicaragua. Wani, 12, 35-47.
_____ 1995a. Recursos pesqueros y sostenibilidad en el Caribe Nicaragüense. Wani, 16, 5-21.
_____ 1995b. Evaluation of sustainable options for transferring the Haulover Fishery Investigation and Demonstration Center. Ayuda Popular Noruega (APN), Managua, Nicaragua. Internal report.

Saila, S.B.; Roedel, P.M. 1980. Stock assessment for tropical small-scale fisheries: proceedings of a University of Rhode Island workshop. International Center for Marine Resource Development, Kingston, RI, USA.

Sánchez R.; Cadima, E.L. 1993. Evaluación de las pesquerías de peneídos de la Costa Caribe Nicaragüense, parte II. Centro de Investigación de Recursos Hidrobiológicos (CIRH), Managua, Nicaragua.

Shiva, V. 1989. Staying alive: women, ecology and development. Zed, London, UK.

Sparr, P.; Ursin, E.; Venema, S.C. 1989. Introduction to tropical fish stock assessment, part 1 (manual). Food and Agriculture Organisation, Rome, Italy. Fisheries technical paper 306/1.

Stoner, A.W. 1986. Community structure of the demersal fish species of Laguna Joyuda, Puerto Rico. Estuaries 9(2), 142-152.

Suman, D., ed. 1994. El ecosistema de manglar en América Latina y la Cuenca del Caribe: su manejo y conservación. Rosentiel School of Marine and Atmospheric Science, University of Miami, Miami, USA.

Systat 1992. Graphics. Version 5.2 Edition manual. Systat, Evanston, IL, USA.

Taylor, B.W. 1962. The status and development of the Nicaraguan pine savannas. Caribbean Forester, 23(1), 21-26.

Thue, E.B.; Rutherford, E.S.; Buker, D.G.. 1982. Age, growth and mortality of the common snook, *Centropomus undecimalis* (Bloch). National Park Service, Homestead, FL, USA. Report T-683.

Tucker, J.W.; Campbell, S.W. 1988. Spawning season for common snook along the east central Florida coast. Florida Scientist, 51(1), 1-6.

Urquhart, G.R. 1997. Disturbance and regeneration of swamp forests in Nicaragua: evidence from ecology and paleoecology. University of Michigan, Ann Arbor, MI, USA. PhD dissertation.

Van Anrooy, R.; Chamorro, E.; Bouwsma, H. 1998. La comercialización del producto pesquero en la Laguna de Perlas 1995–1997. Proyecto DIPAL Convenio Holanda/ Nicaragua. Ministerio de Economía y Desarrollo/Desarrollo de la Pesca, RAAS, Nicaragua. Technical report CO 01.

Van der Hoeven, J.J.; Chamorro, E.; Bouwsma, H. 1995. Informe del desarrollo del programa leasing del proyecto piloto DIPAL. Desarrollo Integral de la Pesca Artesanal en Laguna de Perlas (DIPAL), Pearl Lagoon, Nicaragua. Internal report.

Van der Hoeven, J.J.; Alfaro, E.; Joiner, M.; Blake, E. 1996. Informe de los datos de comercialización de los productos pesqueros en la Cuenca de Laguna de Perlas del año 1995. Pearl Lagoon, Nicaragua. Internal report for Desarrollo Integral de la Pesca Artesanal en Laguna de Perlas (DIPAL)/MEDE-PESCA.

Vandermeer, J. 1990. Los ecosistemas terrestres de la región de Bluefields, Nicaragua. Report for the Centro de Investigaciones y Documentación de la Costa Atlántica (CIDCA). CIDCA, Managua, Nicaragua.
_____ 1991. The political ecology of sustainable development: the Southern Atlantic Coast of Nicaragua. Centennial Review, Spring, 265-294.

Vandermeer, J.; Perfecto, I. 1991. Los bosques del Caribe de Nicaragua: tres años después del Huracán Joan. Wani, 11, 78-102.

Vandermeer, J.; Granzow de la Cerda, I.; Perfecto, I. 1996. La recuperación del bosque continúa en la RAAS. Wani, 20, 38-45.

Vandermeer, J.; Zamora, N.; Yih, K.; Boucher, D. 1990. Regeneración inicial en una selva tropical en la Costa Caribeña de Nicaragua después del huracán Juana. Revista Biología Tropical, 38 (2B), 347-359.

Vendeville, P. 1990. Tropical shrimp fisheries types of fishing gear used and their selectivity. Food and Agriculture Organisation, Rome, Italy. Fisheries technical paper 261 rev. 1.

Vernooy, R. 1992. Starting all over again, making and remaking a living on the Atlantic coast of Nicaragua. University of Wageningen, The Netherlands. PhD dissertation.
_____ 1995. Looking for work: a Nicaraguan Atlantic coastal labour history. European Review of Latin American and Caribbean Studies, 58, 23-44.
_____ 1996. Do you know the python? Moving forward on the participatory research methodology development path. *In* CGIAR systemwide program on participatory research and gender analysis for technology development and institutional innovation. New frontiers in participatory research and gender analysis. Centro Internacional de Agricultura Tropical, Cali, Colombia. pp. 23-36.
_____ 2000. Para una mina de oro se necesita una mina de plata: historiando sobre la Costa Caribe de Nicaragua 1910–1979. Centro de Investigaciones y Documentación de la Costa Atlántica/Universidad Centroamericana (CIDCA/UCA), Managua, Nicaragua.

Vio Grossi, F. 1981. Socio-political implications of participatory research. Convergence, 14, 95-106.

Volpe, A.V. 1959. Aspects of the biology of the common snook, *Centropomus undecimalis* (Bloch) of Southwest Florida. University of Miami Marine Laboratory, Miami, FL, USA.
Walker, T.W. 1997. Introduction: historical setting and important issues. *In* Walker , T.W., ed., Nicaragua without illusions: regime transition and structural adjustment in the 1990s. Scholarly Resources Inc., Wilmington, DE, USA, pp. 1-19.

Weiss, B. 1980. Nutritional adaptation and cultural maladaptation: an evolutionary view. *In* Jerome, N.W.; Kandel, R.F.; Pelto, G.H., ed., Nutritional anthropology: contemporary approaches to diet and culture. Redgrave Publishing, New York, NY, USA. pp. 147-180.

White, A. 1994. Comunidad de Orinoco: un diagnóstico socio-económico. APN and Desarrollo Integral de la Pesca Artesanal en Laguna de Perlas (DIPAL), Bluefields, Nicaragua. Internal report.

White, A.T.; Hale, L.Z.; Renard, Y.; Cortesi, L. ed. 1994. Collaborative and community-based management of coral reefs: lessons from experience. Kumarian Press, West Hartford, CT, USA.

White, N. 1993. La mujer en la pesca: el caso de la comunidad de Orinoco. Central American University, Managua, Nicaragua. BA thesis.

Yañez-Arancibia, A. 1988. Ecology of three sea catfishes (Ariidae) in a tropical coastal ecosystem. Marine Ecology Program Series, 49(3), 215-230.

Yañez-Arancibia, A.; Amezcua-Linares; Day, Jr., J.W. 1980. Fish community structure and function in Terminos Lagoon, a tropical estuary in the southern Gulf of Mexico. *In* Kennedy, V.S., ed., Estuarine perspectives. Academic Press, New York, NY, USA. pp. 465-482.

Yih, K. 1986. Accumulation and women's work in the socialist transformation of agricultural development and equality in conflict. Centro de Investigaciones y Documentación de la Costa Atlántica (CIDCA), Bluefields, Nicaragua. Internal report.

# THE AUTHORS

*David Oliver Bradford* has a BSc degree, with honours in biology, from Trent University. In 1997, he earned a diploma in advanced studies in conflict resolution from Uppsala University, and he is currently pursuing studies toward a master's degree in agricultural development and environmental management at Wye College, University of London. For the past 7 years, he has been conducting research in ecology and natural resource management at the Center for Research and Documentation of the Atlantic Coast of Nicaragua (CIDCA). In 1998, he became CIDCA's executive director.

*Patrick Christie* is a research associate at the School of Marine Affairs, University of Washington, Seattle, USA. He holds an undergraduate degree in zoology from the University of Wisconsin at Madison, a master's degree in conservation biology from the University of Michigan, and a doctorate in resource management and environment from the University of Michigan. He is currently coordinating a project to link Asian academic and coastal management programs with the University of Washington using the Internet and through faculty and student internship exchanges. In the Philippines, Patrick is involved in the evaluation of the social and ecological impacts of the establishment of marine protected areas and integrated coastal management programs. He continues to conduct research on the Caribbean Coast of Nicaragua focusing on the potential of participatory action research for monitoring, planning, and management. Before attending graduate school, Patrick was involved in establishing a community-based marine sanctuary in the Philippines. He is also an associate editor of the journal, *Coastal Management*.

*Ray Garth* is a forest technician, who graduated from the Instituto Technológico Forestal in Estelí, Nicaragua, and one of the founding members of CIDCA. Since 1994, he has worked with CAMPlab as a community investigator and forest technician. Ray also works as a dendrologist during the annual tropical ecology course organized by CIDCA in cooperation with the University of Michigan and, recently, with the University of Guelph.

*Bonifacio González* has a high-school diploma from the Instituto Tecnológico Cristóbal Colón, Bluefields, Nicaragua. He has worked as a community investigator for CAMPlab since 1995.

*Mark Hostetler* is currently pursuing studies toward a doctorate in geography at York University, Toronto, Canada, focusing on political ecology, the political economy of development, and applied sustainability. He has completed master's degrees in Latin American studies and political science at Simon Fraser University and a bachelor's degree in political science and geography at Wilfrid Laurier University. In 1998, he spent several months in the Pearl Lagoon area carrying out fieldwork for his master's thesis.

*Oswaldo Morales*, who was born in La Fe, Nicaragua, graduated with a certificate in private accounting and bookkeeping from the Pearl Lagoon Institute. He is currently involved in a bachelor's program at the Faculty of Education Science at the Universidad de las Regiones Autónomas de la Costa Caribe de Nicaragua. He has been part of the CAMPlab staff for 4 years, both as project administrator and community investigator.

**Roberto Rigby** is a biologist with a particular interest in coastal ecosystems. He studied at the National Autonomous University of Nicaragua and at the Higher Fisheries School in Havana. He is currently enrolled in a number of courses in marine biology at the Centre for Marine Research in Havana.

**Bertha Simmons**, who was born in Bluefields, graduated as a social worker from the Central American University in Nicaragua. She took postgraduate courses in conflict resolution at the European Peace University in Austria and on gender in development at Puntos de Encuentro, in Managua, Nicaragua. She has been coordinator of the CAMPlab project since 1998.

**Eduardo Tinkam** is one of CAMPlab's community investigators. He was born and raised in Haulover, where he worked as an elementary school teacher, as the director of an elementary school, and as supervisor of school programs. Born and raised in Haulover, he has a wealth of knowledge about the region, its people, and its resources.

**Gabriel Vega** is an ecologist, who graduated from the Central American University in Managua in 1995. Gabriel worked as a researcher with CAMPlab for 3 years. During this time, he created and maintained the project's database.

**Ronnie Vernooy** is a rural sociologist trained at the Agricultural University of Wageningen, the Netherlands. His research interests include natural resource management, agricultural biodiversity, organizational development, and participatory (action) research. Since 1992, he has been a program officer at the International Development Research Centre in Ottawa, Canada. He has a special affinity for Nicaragua where he carried out field research in 1985–86, 1988–91, and 1997–98, both in the Pacific region of Matagalpa and on the Atlantic coast. He coauthored and edited *Cómo vamos a sobrevivir nosotros?* (How are we going to survive?), a book about how people of the Nicaraguan coast deal with the ups and downs of the economy and how they coped with the devastating impact of Hurricane Joan in 1988. He also wrote and compiled a new book about the history of the Atlantic coast: *Para una mina de oro se necesita una mina de plata: historiando sobre la Costa Caribe de Nicaragua 1910–1979*, which was published by CIDCA-UCA.

**Noreen White**, who was born in Bonanza, in the Northern Autonomous Atlantic Region, is currently CIDCA's executive subdirector, based in Bluefields. She holds degrees from the Central American University, the University of Michigan, and the University of Guelph. She has been with CIDCA since 1989, carrying out research on women's roles in the fisheries sector, socioeconomic development on the Atlantic coast, tropical ecology, biodiversity conservation, and environmental education.

# About the publishers

The **Centro de Investigaciones y Documentación de la Costa Atlántica (CIDCA)** is the first and only specialized research organization focusing on Nicaragua's Caribbean or Atlantic coastal region. Since 1981, CIDCA has promoted research and the publication of information about Nicaragua's Caribbean region. The centre is affiliated with the Central American University.

CIDCA promotes development throughout Nicaragua's Caribbean coast, contributing to solutions for specific problems with studies, research, and consultancies meant to strengthen the autonomy process. CIDCA aims to produce work of high scientific standards while disseminating the results of such works in publications accessible to all sectors of Costeño society.

CIDCA's main contributions to date include:

- Designing, planning, and monitoring essential aspects of the Atlantic coast autonomy process.
- Introducing the bilingual education program in Nicaragua and preserving native languages.
- Expanding the collective memory of Atlantic coast residents through the identification and recovery of primary historical documents previously held in other countries, including England, Spain, Jamaica, Belize, Germany, and the United States.
- Conducting ecological studies and environmental research on the Nicaraguan Caribbean coast, including a 10-year monitoring project on the impact of Hurricane Joan on the forests of southeastern Nicaragua, for which CIDCA won the 1997 Semper Virens award granted by the Ministry of the Environment and Natural Resources of Nicaragua for outstanding contribution to environmental conservation.
- Addressing the historical demands of the indigenous communities through analysis of land tenure within the Atlantic coast region.
- Publishing *Wani*, a scientific journal devoted to the study of the Nicaragua's Atlantic coast.

The **International Development Research Centre (IDRC)** is committed to building a sustainable and equitable world. IDRC funds developing-world researchers, thus enabling the people of the South to find their own solutions to their own problems. IDRC also maintains information networks and forges linkages that allow Canadians and their developing-world partners to benefit equally from a global sharing of knowledge. Through its actions, IDRC is helping others to help themselves.

IDRC Books publishes research results and scholarly studies on global and regional issues related to sustainable and equitable development. As a specialist in development literature, IDRC Books contributes to the body of knowledge on these issues to further the cause of global understanding and equity. IDRC publications are sold through its head office in Ottawa, Canada, as well as by IDRC's agents and distributors around the world. The full catalogue is available at: http://www.idrc.ca/booktique.

Este producto fue impreso
en los Talleres Gráficos Offset
de la Universidad Centroamericana (UCA)